Creative Approaches to Imp
Participation

WITHDRAWN from collection

Introducing creativity into the classroom is a challenge for governments and teachers. Employers around the world are increasingly interested in people who can think and work in a creative fashion. Families and communities need people who are self-reliant and able to take risks, express and speak up for themselves and act independently. In recent years there has been a drive to make experiences at school more exciting, relevant, challenging and dynamic for all young people.

Creative Approaches to Improving Participation explores imaginative and creative ways to involve young people and children as stakeholders in their education. It looks at how they have actively participated in their own learning; transforming classrooms, curricula, school environments and teaching practices. Promoting reflection on current student–teacher–school relationships, links between home and school and between school and the wider world, the contributions within this book illustrate how the active engagement of students can lead to greater confidence, self-reliance and risk taking; skills essential for a successful post-school career. Through an exploration of students' current inclusion in school life, this book provides:

- a study of key issues and debates surrounding student participation;
- ideas for increasing student participation and motivation for learning;
- case studies from a range of creative learning projects with analysis of their achievements and challenges;
- guidance on the creation of active, relevant and effective pedagogies;
- practical suggestions for reflective practice and CPD.

A functional, accessible guide to creatively increasing students' participation, this book is valuable reading for all practising and trainee teachers, school managers and school leaders working with young people in education.

Helen Manchester is Visiting Research Fellow in the Education and Social Research Institute at Manchester Metropolitan University, UK.

Creative Teaching/Creative Schools Series

Series Editors: Pat Thomson, Julian Sefton-Green and Naranee Ruthra-Rajan

Creative Approaches to Improving Participation

Giving learners a say

Edited by Helen Manchester

 Routledge
Taylor & Francis Group

LONDON AND NEW YORK

First published 2012
by Routledge
2 Park Square, Milton Park, Abingdon, Oxon OX14 4RN

Simultaneously published in the USA and Canada
by Routledge
711 Third Avenue, New York, NY 10017

Routledge is an imprint of the Taylor & Francis Group, an informa business

British Library Cataloguing in Publication Data
A catalogue record for this book is available from the British Library

Library of Congress Cataloging in Publication Data
Creative approaches to improving participation: giving learners a say/[edited by] Helen Manchester.
  p. cm. – (Creative teaching/creative schools)
  1. Student-centered learning. 2. Active learning. 3. Creative teaching. 4. Motivation in education. I. Manchester, Helen.
  LB1027.23.C725 2011
  370.15′4–dc22   2011009022

ISBN: 978-0-415-57620-8 (hbk)
ISBN: 978-0-415-57621-5 (pbk)
ISBN: 978-0-203-81816-9 (ebk)

Typeset in Galliard
by HWA Text and Data Management, London

Printed and bound in Great Britain by the MPG Books Group

Contents

Illustrations

Contributors

Rehmuna Begum was once a very shy Year 7 student at Waverley School in Birmingham who decided to join the school's Youth Panel in the hope of finding like-minded people and her voice. Now in Year 10 she has found her voice verbally (we can't keep her quiet!), through art work and now through writing. She wants all young people to have the confidence to have their voices heard. Rehmuna aspires to continue to express herself through a career in photographic journalism.

Rachel Carter is an experienced creative consultant based in the West Midlands who has had the privilege of working with many of the region's arts and cultural organisations and schools. She has six years of teaching experience in two inner-city Birmingham schools and 13 years' experience in working in a range of arts, cultural and education settings. She is also very proud to be Chair of Governors at The Dame Ellen Pinsent School.

Debra Cleeland teaches at Edgewick Primary School in Coventry where she has played a pivotal role in pedagogical and curriculum development. For the last three years she has been seconded to work with Creative Partnerships as a pupil voice consultant in both primary and secondary settings. She is passionate about creative teaching as a dynamic vehicle for activating the intellect, emotions and imagination of young people.

Sally Cox is currently Deputy Principal of a large Leicestershire upper school in Wigston. She is a teacher of geography with a diverse role. Her responsibilities have included care and guidance, community and parental engagement, directing the college specialism, children in care, continuing professional development and performance management, developing student voice, policy development and feeder school liaison. She became involved with Creative Partnerships in 2008 and led a successful application to become a Creative Partnerships Change School. This opportunity enabled Sally to combine her key strengths in promoting creativity across the college.

Ben Edwards coordinates creativity and music at Three Ways Special School in Bath. He began his career as a primary teacher and discovered his passion for teaching students with special educational needs whilst working in northern Japan. On returning to the UK he trained to become an educational psychologist with particular interest in researching self-esteem and its impact on pupils' experiences of learning. Since joining the team at Three Ways, Ben has been heavily involved in the development of multisensory immersive learning experiences and Forest Schools approaches to learning.

Mathilda Joubert is a consultant, trainer and researcher in creativity, innovation and the management of change. She works nationally and internationally with organisations from across the business, arts, education, government and voluntary sectors.

Sarah Joubert is an Advanced Skills Teacher and Head of Art at Waverley School in Birmingham. She has six years of teaching experience in inner-city Birmingham schools and is passionate about the importance of creative teaching and learning for our young people. Prior to embarking on her teaching career she worked in costume for theatre, film and television in both London and New York. She would like to thank the students of Stagedoor Manor Performing Arts in New York whose energy, honesty and creativity led her into teaching.

Asima Qureshi was deputy head at Dunkirk Primary School for 12 years and is now working part time as a consultant for the school. She is the School of Creativity co-ordinator at the school as well as managing their innovative international linking work which utilises creative methods to build dialogue between Dunkirk and schools in Pakistan, Spain and the Lebanon. Before this she was a class teacher for many years. She is passionate about making the curriculum relevant for all and helping the school to embody community cohesion in order to support children's learning.

Parmjit Sagoo is a drama practitioner and creative advisor, working within education and community settings. Parmjit has been lead artist and creative agent for Dunkirk Primary for over eight years, supporting the school in embedding creativity and global citizenship at the heart of the school community. She is particularly interested in global citizenship, community cohesion, international linking and the therapeutic potential of the creative process. She is currently studying for an MA in drama therapy and is researching how yoga, visualisation and meditation can be part of the learning process (for teachers and children).

Claire Simpson is an artist/educator working predominantly through collaboration with schools, community groups, other artists and venues, creating work through projects, commissions, residencies and training. She has worked with people of all ages, but particularly with early-years groups, primary school aged children and people with learning disabilities. Claire is driven by a love of the natural world and is a level 3 Forest School leader. She draws inspiration from the ethos of Reggio Emilia and believes that we all use our imaginations and creative instincts to play, learn, explore, communicate and to make sense of ourselves and our surroundings.

Neil Small studied for his PGCE at Brighton and has since worked in primary schools in the south-east of England. He is currently head teacher at Castledown Community Primary School in Hastings where he is working with the children and teachers to increase creative approaches to learning through building up pupil voice initiatives in the school.

Ruth Turnbull is a West Midlands based textile artist who has extensive experience of working on collaborative arts projects and workshops in primary and secondary schools. She uses traditional textile techniques to develop curriculum based arts activities. Ruth has four years' teaching experience and also works as a freelance textile designer for the interior/furnishings national and international commercial market.

Series introduction

We live in creative times. As political aspiration, as economic driver, as a manifesto for school reform and curriculum change, the desire for creativity can be found across the developed world in policy pronouncements and academic research. But creativity in schools can mean many things: turning classrooms into more exciting experiences, curriculum into more thoughtful challenges, teachers into different kinds of instructors, assessment into more authentic processes and putting young people's voice at the heart of learning. In general, these aspirations are motivated by two key concerns – to make experience at school more exciting, relevant, challenging and dynamic; and ensuring that young people are able to contribute to the creative economy which will underpin growth in the twenty-first century.

Transforming these common aspirations into informed practice is not easy. Yet there are programmes, projects and initiatives which have consistently attempted to offer change and transformation. There are significant creativity programmes in many parts of the world, including France, Norway, Canada, South Korea, Australia and the United States of America. The English programme, Creative Partnerships (www.creative-partnerships.com) is the largest of these and this series of books draws on its experience and expertise.

This book, *Creative Approaches to Improving Participation: Giving Learners a Say* is published as part of a series of books, *Creative Teaching/Creative Schools*. The series is written for headteachers, curriculum co-ordinators and classroom practitioners who are interested in creative learning and teaching. Each book offers principles for changing classroom and school practice and stimulus material for CPD sessions. The emphasis is on practical, accessible studies from real schools, framed by jargon-free understandings of key issues and the principles found in more academic studies. Each volume contains six detailed 'case studies' written by practising teachers and other creative practitioners each describing a project they have introduced in their schools. These stories are complemented by accounts from learners themselves, making clear the benefit and value of these approaches to changing learning.

What is creative learning?

When educators talk about creative learning they generally mean teaching which allows students to use their imaginations, have ideas, generate multiple possible solutions to problems, communicate in a variety of media and in general 'think outside the box'. They may also mean practices in which children and young people show that they have the capacities to assess and improve work, sustain effort on a project for a long period of time, exceed what they thought was possible and work well with others to combine ideas and approaches. Some may extend the notion to include projects and approaches which allow young people to apply their creativity through making choices about what and how they will learn, negotiating about curriculum and involvement in generating possibilities for and making decisions about school priorities and directions.

But while there may be commonalities about what creative learning looks like as and in students' behaviours, there may also be profound differences. The notion of creativity may be associated with particular subjects, such as those that go under the umbrella term of the arts, in which generating new, odd and interesting perspectives on familiar topics is valued and rewarded. Or it may be seen as integral to science where habits of transforming curiosity into hypotheses have a long history. Or it may be connected to business and the goal of schooling students to have strongly entrepreneurial dispositions and capacities. These interpretations – and many more – are all possible and legitimate understandings of creativity and creative learning.

Although the term 'creative learning' may be new and fashionable, it draws on older knowledge and values which have helped give it legitimacy and which frame its current meaning (see *The Routledge International Handbook of Creative Learning* and *Researching Creative Learning, Methods and Issues*).

We have expressed our understanding of Creative Learning as a series of 'manifesto' principles. They underpin all the volumes in this series.

Students' creative learning depends on a quality of education where:

- all young people from every kind of background are equally recognised as being creative;
- learning engages young people in serious, meaningful, relevant, imaginative and challenging activities and tasks;
- young people are respected for their knowledge, experience and capabilities;
- young people have an individual and collective right to actively shape their education;
- teachers have the power to support, adapt and evaluate learning experiences for students exercising their professional judgement;
- schools invest in teacher learning;
- schools build partnerships with creative individuals and organisations;
- schools enable young people to participate fully in social and cultural worlds;
- families and local communities can play an inspiring and purposeful role in young people's learning.

Creative approaches to improving participation

This book's theme is student participation. It explores imaginative and creative ways to involve young people and children as stakeholders in their education. It offers ways of giving a 'voice' to school students of all ages and engaging them in a range of projects. The book also explores some of the contradictions and tensions inherent in ambitions to 'give' students voice and shows through case studies how aspirations to share authority in the classroom need careful and thoughtful preparation and implementation. Above all, it makes the case that finding ways to make students more equal can be both challenging and rewarding and ultimately lead to transformations not only in classrooms but across whole schools.

Pat Thomson
Julian Sefton-Green
Naranee Ruthra-Rajan

Acknowledgements

I would like to thank the teachers and creative practitioners who have contributed to this book for their hard work, patience and willingness to share their experiences. Thanks also to the photographers who provided the images used throughout the book, especially to Ruth Turnbull for the majority of the photographs in Chapter 2 and Claire Simpson for the photographs in Chapter 5. Thanks also to Julian Sefton-Green for his intellectual support and encouragement throughout and Naranee Ruthra-Rajan for her editing.

Findings from the research project conducted by Sara Bragg and myself concerning 'Youth voice in the work of Creative Partnerships' have been invaluable in putting this book together and I would like to thank Sara for her rigour, and the intellectual and personal support she has provided throughout.

1

Introduction

Helen Manchester

Chapter overview

This book is about creative approaches to giving learners, teachers and other staff members a say in schools. This introduction aims to establish some key ideas and terminology that will be taken up and exemplified in the subsequent case studies.

The terms 'children' and 'children and young people' are used in this book to refer to all those aged 11 and under, and 'young people' for those aged 12 and above. Although legally the term 'child' in the UK refers to those under 18 (Masson, 2004) this does not take account of the differences between, for instance, infants and teenagers. Throughout the book, authors have therefore included specific ages of the children and young people in their projects.

Participation in this book is taken to mean young people's active and direct involvement in school matters (although alternative understandings are discussed below). Participation is understood as an inclusive process in which children and young people are seen as valued and respected contributors – with the right to express views, be heard and to take part in activities and decisions that affect them (Bragg and Fielding, 2003).

A key principle underpinning this book is that schools and classrooms are not 'containers' but are shaped by wider factors including policy and also the experiences, skills and knowledge that young people and adults bring with them. Therefore, when setting up creative participation activities with young people staff might ask themselves (and the young people) questions such as:

- Who are the pupils/young people? What are they interested in outside school? What knowledge, experiences and resources do they bring into school? What are they good at?
- What kind of neighbourhood do the young people live in? What opportunities do they have in this neighbourhood? What learning happens in this neighbourhood?
- Which local and global communities do young people have links with?

■ What activities in school/outside school do young people generally find most engaging, exciting, thought provoking?

These questions permeate the rest of this book and suggest the strong link between young people's creative participation in schools and adult recognition of and understandings of young people's cultures, lives and experiences.

The introduction begins by looking at the case for student participation and voice in schools, exploring what student participation has looked like in schools up to now. It then examines the potential of creative approaches to participation, challenging common assumptions around this work. Finally it explores the key practices that have been found to be most important in creative participation initiatives and suggests some critical questions that can be applied to develop successful creative participation projects.

Why student participation?

At this juncture in the twenty-first century it is increasingly accepted that young people should have a say and be consulted about their places and spaces of learning. Indeed young people are increasingly being asked their opinions on a range of issues concerning their lives; for example about local and national policy frameworks, the redesign of environments (both inside and outside school), on the delivery of arts and cultural events, urban regeneration projects and by marketers with reference to the commercial worlds of product design and marketing strategies (Bragg, 2010).

A number of laws, policy discourses and academic studies support, encourage and demand this participatory turn, for example: the United Nations Convention on the Rights of the Child (UNCRC, 1989); government policy agendas, such as 'Every Child Matters' in the UK (DfES, 2003); a recent emphasis on citizenship in schools and neighbourhoods (Osler, 2000; Osler and Starkey, 2003). How we take up these resources affects our view of young people's participation and therefore the practices that we design around young people's participation in school.

The history of schooling shows how the physical layout of a school segregated young people and adults. Children sat in classrooms at desks arranged in rows that faced the front, whilst the teacher stood at the front of the room, supervising and admonishing. As Foucault (1977) suggests, within this system of ordering, the boundary between adulthood and childhood became fixed. As 'school' became an increasingly large part of young people's lives they and other children were also segregated from other institutions and practices and therefore constructed as 'different' to others.

Demands are made on schools to seek the views of young people (Office for Standards in Education – Ofsted) and to consult pupils about decisions affecting them (Education Act 2002). In addition the 2003 government Green Paper, 'Every Child Matters' (DfES, 2003), recognises the importance of children having a say in developing policies that affect them directly. Parallel demands have been made for schools to foreground creativity and creative learning, for example in policy documents such as Excellence and Enjoyment (2003). There are overlaps between youth participation and creativity which are often presented as ways that schools can meet the challenges of the twenty-first century, for instance through improving the quality of learning, increasing student and staff motivation or changing a school's ethos.

These requirements, together with changing notions of childhood, have led to what many have called a 'participatory turn' in schools alongside a growing focus on creative approaches to learning. However, Jeffrey and Craft (2008) suggest that tensions can arise when teachers are encouraged to take risks and foster creativity whilst at the same time they are subject to a strong accountability regime. We return to these tensions throughout this review but also within the chapters of this book.

What has 'student participation' looked like up to now?

Student participation projects may be developed for a number of reasons, such as:

- School improvement
  - improving teaching and learning;
  - monitoring and evaluating new curriculum and other initiatives;
  - contributing to processes of school re-design, or restructuring.
- Modelling and enacting democracy (a citizenship agenda)
  - helping to establish a more democratic school system;
  - supporting the principles of citizenship education;
  - contributing to the personal and social development of pupils.

(Adapted from Fielding and Bragg, 2003)

- Personal development
  - Developing young people's skills and capacities as learners/as citizens.

Motives for developing such activities clearly matter and range from pragmatic concerns such as improving attendance and exam results to more democratic ambitions to make schools more equitable for all, or making curriculum more relevant to young people's everyday lives and communities. Of course, in practice, motives for participation work are often mixed and sometimes confused. In the next section I take some of the main drivers for student participation initiatives in schools, and examine how these drivers might be turned into projects.

School improvement

Partly in response to a growing unease about young people's disengagement from school, policy makers and practitioners have looked to students to find out more about what they enjoy about school and what they would like to see changed. Students here are encouraged to acquire a language for talking about teaching and learning; and participation is often related to involvement in formal school decision making.

Initiatives range from consultation exercises such as student questionnaires, which may mirror consumer style surveys, to more elaborate programmes that involve students as researchers in their school. Projects may focus on individualised approaches, for example where students are asked to reflect on their own learning and 'take responsibility' for its success or failure. At other times the focus is more collective, involving the school community reflecting on their school, in dialogue with each other (Flutter and Rudduck, 2004).

It is in this discussion work that schools are able to recognise and take into account the views of young people, teachers and other adults in the school, acknowledging the interdependence of different groups in school. Therefore it is important to remember in any student voice approaches that teachers, parents and others involved in schools also have views and that we should not romanticise learner voices and consider them more 'true' or authentic. In addition 'young people' are not a homogenous group, so we should not assume that one learner or a group of learners may be able to 'speak for' others.

The citizenship agenda and democratic schools

A focus on 'citizenship' in schools has helped to foreground young people's participation. The push here has been on young people being actively involved in their schools and wider communities rather than passively acquiring information about citizenship. Osler (2000) suggests that consulting young people in this way helps them to develop skills of cooperation, compromise and recognition of difference. A 'citizenship' agenda may also focus on critical local and global questions about the kind of world we want to live in, and about our rights and responsibilities as citizens. Participation here may extend beyond the school and encourage community and/or social activism and organising.

Some suggest that student participation work may model and enact more democratic principles in schools, for instance modelling less hierarchical relationships and more democratic forms of decision making. These 'democratic principles' are contested but might include:

- *All* pupils in the school contributing to decision making in positions of governance and policy making, in classrooms and learning. Student leadership is diffuse and extends to many.
- The need for structural equity – all children and young people have equal access to all programmes in school. The school seeks to include, rather than exclude.
- Recognising sources of inequity, and debating them through systems of 'deliberative democracy'.
- Students and teachers seeing themselves as part of the world – working with and on the production of important knowledge related to active social and cultural participation in local and global worlds.
- Making classroom practice more open and participatory.

- The creation of a positive environment for learning in which students can: take risks; feel safe; make meaning; develop a sense of competence, belonging and usefulness; experience excitement and ownership; and work creatively.

(Adapted from Thomson, 2007; Fielding, 2010)

In practice these democratic principles may be hard to instil. Arnot (2004) suggests that teachers are often under pressure to support government agendas that may not correspond to their own priorities, or those of young people in the school. However, projects in which young people take up positions of governance in schools, where they are involved in decision making and play an active role in initiating, delivering and evaluating school initiatives are becoming more common. These approaches certainly contrast with those that see 'citizenship' as something that can be learnt passively – potentially involving some 'political' learning.

Personal development model

Skills that are often associated with student participation work are those identified as useful for future employment, such as time management, public speaking and running meetings. Consulting students about their learning may also enable them to become better 'self reflective' learners (Fielding and Bragg, 2003) – a skill seen as essential in a lifelong learning society. Commonly listed benefits include increased self-respect, competence, confidence, trust in adults and themselves, self-esteem, social inclusion, sense of responsibility for taking increased control over aspects of their lives, understanding of decision-making processes, and fun and enjoyment. You will see how these benefits may be brought about later in the case studies. For example, in Chapter 6 the young men involved in the project at Three Ways School develop their confidence and trust in adults, and their own self-esteem whilst having fun during the project. However, we also note that the personal benefits of consultation are often limited to the small numbers of young people who take part, and therefore the benefits for all of the other young people in their schools are not always clear (Davies *et al.*, 2006).

Degrees of involvement

The motives for beginning a participation activity then do affect how projects play out and what kinds of benefits young people might get from them. These motives may also affect the degree of involvement of the young people within the project. Many authors have tried to map or model these.

Some popular models to design and evaluate student participation have concentrated only on the role of the young people involved – such as those by Hart (1992) and Flutter and Rudduck (2004) (see Appendix at the end of the book, pp. 99–108). In a recent model Michael Fielding (2010) examines partnerships between adults and students in schools and other educational contexts instead. He suggests six forms of interaction between adults and young people:

- students as data source – in which staff utilise information about student progress and well-being;
- students as active respondents – in which staff invite student dialogue and discussion to deepen learning/professional decisions;
- students as co-enquirers – in which staff take a lead role with high-profile, active student support;
- students as knowledge creators – in which students take lead roles with active staff support;
- students as joint authors – in which students and staff decide on a joint course of action together;
- intergenerational learning as participatory democracy – in which there is a shared commitment to/responsibility for the common good.

Fielding admits that school structures and relationship divides common to school systems often mitigate against the latter modes in his framework; however he does provide evidence of them working in school settings. In this book examples of these latter modes can be seen particularly in Chapter 5 where teachers and artists work with children as co-authors in their creative learning project. Other examples also appear in other chapters.

You might want to consider using this model or others (see the Appendix at the end of the book) to reflect on the case studies in this book, as well as on your own participation projects in schools.

Participation outcomes and critiques

Student participation can be a positive force in schools that works to change relations between adults and young people and gives young people a greater say in shaping their education. However the field of student participation hides a diverse and complex alliance of reform agendas. For example the Labour government's use of the personalisation agenda, linking 'voice' with 'choice' may align voice with the marketisation and commodification of education – where students are asked to make choices as clients rather than being asked about their opinions as learners. As a result of the different motives for student participation activities, it has been suggested that at times educators may be using student voice work as an additional mechanism of control – for instance, aligning pupil consultation with a narrow focus on school improvement targets defined by adults. Within these 'school improvement' projects there may be a focus on 'evidence based' voice where students develop skills related to research and 'academic' training – writing questionnaires, surveys, or interviewing. These processes are often designed by adults, and activities involve small numbers of young people being trained up to participate in adult orientated processes (e.g. involving formal meetings and written reports). It is suggested that they therefore often fail to engage with students' real concerns and own preferences for communicating ideas (Bragg, Manchester and Faulkner, 2009).

In fact, research into student participation activities provides mixed results – a gap between rhetoric and reality. There are some positive signs; for example,

Morgan (2007) suggests that when teachers seriously consider pupils' views this can be the basis for new kinds of classroom climates and relationships. However, others have found that where adults do not seem to respond to or take student views seriously, young people themselves may question adult motivations leading them to lose faith in the processes of student voice and consultation (Whitty and Wisby, 2007).

Creative approaches and participation

This book suggests that creative approaches, for instance where creative practitioners[1] such as dancers, visual artists or multimedia artists work alongside teachers, or when teachers adapt their own teaching to encourage creative learning, may help student participation work in schools. As you will see in the case studies, such approaches often require a significant level of involvement from young people and new kinds of relationships between learners and teachers.

It is important to say here that creativity has been variously understood. As Banaji *et al.* (2010) argue, there is no one definition of creativity but rather a range of 'rhetorics' that surround creativity. The manner in which individual schools take up these rhetorics will affect their creative participation projects. You will see this more clearly as you read through the chapters: for instance at Dunkirk Primary School creative participation is aligned with the democratic and the political; whereas at West Rise Junior School the Room 13 model draws more on a discourse of creative professionalism and social enterprise. This book encourages you to think through your own understandings of creativity, reflecting on the various effects this understanding may have on your own creative participation activities.

The benefits of creative approaches to developing participation

This section describes eight of the general benefits of adopting creative approaches and working with creative practitioners on participation activities. I suggest that such approaches can potentially challenge some of the more problematic, or co-opted models of student voice in schools.

First, creative practitioners often bring *pedagogies and methods* from their experiences in the informal sector, or in early years settings, to their work in schools. These methods, originating, for instance in community arts and youth work or from early childhood pedagogies abroad (such as Reggio Emilia[2] or Forest School approaches[3]), often foreground more participatory ways of working with young people and may encourage teachers, for instance, to adopt more flexible approaches to planning, enabling students to shape content.

Second, creative approaches and practitioners may also work from and with *pupils' existing knowledge and interests,* responding to issues and questions they bring into school and integrating these topics into project led learning that becomes cross curricular. This kind of approach may encourage work that moves away from strictly timetabled slots for specific subjects and involves the integration of opportunities for students to decide what and how they learn (although student decisions concerning the 'what' of learning may be less easy to enable where curriculum is strictly defined).

Third, creative approaches are also often linked with more '*authentic' forms of expression* for young people – for example, through being more closely linked to youth culture, or drawing on their own involvement in participatory digital cultures. In this way learning becomes more meaningful and engaging. Of course teachers are also able to draw on young people's own resources in this way, but may find creative practitioners provide a catalyst in offering their own tools, skills and resources as a starting point.

Fourth, *working in partnership* with creative practitioners, with adequate time for observation, reflection and experimentation is often an effective way of increasing teacher confidence and enthusiasm for creative approaches. In addition, as creative practitioners work alongside teachers they may also model partnership working and dialogue for young people. Creative practitioners often bring fresh perspectives into schools through their particular professional practice. For example, they might highlight the importance of space and environment in learning or encourage others to pay attention to 'the visual' in an activity or learning space.

Fifth, creative approaches often necessitate *different tools and resources* in the classroom. These may be new media technologies, textiles, real clay, sharp knives, or visual representations. Along with the tools and resources come different approaches to the use of these tools – for instance requiring young people to be more responsible for their own actions in using potentially dangerous tools, or placing young people in a different position of authority in relation to adults and their learning environments. These approaches can be in tension with the focus on child protection in schools and can lead to some interesting discussions and reflection on these increasingly 'taken-for-granted' aspects of school culture. This may challenge adult views of what young people and children are capable of and encourage young people to take more responsibility for their own environments of learning. This is exemplified in Forest School approaches where children from the age of three build fires, use tools and are encouraged to explore natural environments.

Sixth, the very fact that creative practitioners are in schools can increase students' access to cultural resources and networks. For instance, their presence in school may suggest *different possible identities* for young people that may connect with their own experiences and/or cultures. Working with professionals who are not teachers may also offer new approaches to learning or different possible futures to young people. Teachers may also be encouraged to experiment with different identities, for instance by drawing on their own identities and interests outside school, and this often results in increased teacher satisfaction.

Seventh, creative approaches will often involve young people going *out of school* and may involve schools and young people engaging with the local cultural sector, for instance art galleries, museums and creative industries, or with their local neighbourhood in other ways. This kind of work often links with notions of active citizenship for instance as young people are encouraged to build new connections with the world or even new identities as artists in their own right (see Waverley case study Chapter 2). Creative approaches that link with nature may also help in breaking down traditional boundaries between school and the outside world (Jeffrey and Woods, 2003).

Eighth, creative expression offers young people opportunities to move away from traditional, academic modes of collecting and presenting data, which are often features of student participation approaches in schools. This more *'hands-on' approach* might involve participatory video, drama, role-play and student radio or podcasts instead of questionnaires and interviews, to research and present student perspectives. This may also increase their appeal and enable a wider range of students to participate. For instance, a dance and drama artist described her work with young people,

> We are having conversations but it is not about how articulate they are, it is about them voicing their opinions and their thoughts, using drama and dance work, there are moments where you can express yourself and it is not about the language that you use or how many syllables were in the words that you use.
>
> (cited in Bragg, Manchester and Faulkner, 2009, p. 48)

In Special Schools, working with creative practitioners may enable students to express views and responses in different and non-verbal ways.

Some caveats

However, there are a number of myths that surround creative approaches. First is the principle that creative approaches are inherently more participatory and inclusive, that they are more likely to involve collaborative activity, or that creative practitioners are naturally more disposed to participatory approaches. In fact, it is not helpful to set up creative practitioners as somehow 'better than' teachers at managing participation – rather, as the following chapters describe, it is often a partnership between practitioners and teachers that works best. Also it should perhaps be noted that creative practitioners often work in different circumstances from teachers, for example with smaller groups of students and in different timescales (for example a whole morning or a whole day on one project). They certainly do not experience the same pressure as teachers in raising attainment or achieving prescribed outcomes.

Teachers do sometimes experience doubt over the integration of creative approaches into classrooms, as can be seen in Chapter 3 at Edgewick Primary School. Often this is to do with teacher identities in relationship to the word 'creative' – for instance many teachers often say that they are 'not creative' or feel uncomfortable about moving away from tried and tested methods that they have found relatively successful. There may therefore be a need to raise teacher confidence and skills in using these kind of approaches, which may take some time. Also young people's own insecurities around their capacity to 'be creative' should not be ignored.

Key practices in creative youth participation

All the case study schools were committed to the belief that creativity was the key to engaging young people in participation activities. However, many of the themes that come out of these case studies may be equally applicable to other types of participation activities.

Relations

Sociologists suggest that rather than thinking in terms of '*the* child' a diversity of *childhoods* should be recognised since children's experiences vary with their ethnicity, social class and gender (James and Prout, 1997). It is therefore important to consider how groups of young people get along with each other and how their rivalries and allegiances may affect their participation. This dimension is often neglected in evaluating such work. You may find that antagonisms arising from educational practices (such as ability setting) and youth cultural affiliations may be powerful, negative, factors in young people's learning experience, and some participation initiatives potentially exacerbate such divisions (Bragg, Manchester and Faulkner, 2009).

Research and practice on participation work in schools has tended to focus on the young people themselves rather than considering the implications for adult roles in schools. However, this book suggests a refocus on 'intergenerationality' and on listening to the voices of young people *and* adults. In this way schools may move beyond persistent hierarchical structures and towards a model where, 'children's need for support and their capacity to be powerful social actors can co-exist; in which adults' need to learn new skills and their capacity to provide responsibility and care are seen as compatible.' (Facer, 2008, p.10). The support that adults supply within creative participation projects is a theme that runs through all the chapters of this volume.

Identities

Participation activities may challenge adult expectations of young people and of their capacity to engage in decision-making or in curriculum and other central school processes. Where views are challenged in this way, projects are more likely to lead to increased involvement of young people in wider decision making in school.

In this book all young people are seen as bringing valuable experiences, understanding and knowledge into school. From this perspective those leading creative participation projects in schools should consider their own beliefs about young people as well as the prevalent image of young people held in the school. The successful integration of creative approaches may work best where there is a shared ethos and commitment from adults to working alongside young people and co-producing learning with them.

New ways of working may also enable young people and their teachers to take on new identities, both within the project space but concurrently within wider school practices. For example, more participatory ways of working may challenge more traditional adult/teacher roles in school.

Attention to teacher identities and teacher 'voice' is an important consideration in young people's participation initiatives. This involves developing teachers' sense of professional competence, encouraging collaboration and reflective practice. A focus on teacher voice can enable teachers to make more profound (and potentially risky) changes to their pedagogy and relationships with students – perhaps through the implementation of creative and participatory approaches. Professional development programmes feature in many of the case studies that follow – suggesting that creative approaches to participation may thrive where time and resources are provided to increase teachers' professional skills and confidence.

Space, context and participation

Creative practitioners often work hard to create spaces that feel different from school, and encourage young people to leave their school based identities behind them. They might do this through humanistic approaches to learning – where they encourage young people to explore their feelings and emotions in a 'safe' environment (see Rogers, 1970). Other approaches include changing the environment in more tangible ways through bringing in cushions, drawing curtains around a space or playing music. Often the spaces created will suggest different rules and conventions concerning the dynamics of interpersonal and power relationships between young people and between young people and adults.

However, creative participation programmes that are set up outside or independent of the usual practices and structures of school may be problematic. For instance teachers may only be involved at a superficial level or not at all. Others in school may not be 'witnesses' to change and the school context may not support the new identities and relationships formed in these 'outside' spaces. Opportunities for integration and dialogue clearly need to be planned for and conscientiously maintained to increase the likelihood of benefits resulting from such work (Bragg, Manchester and Faulkner, 2009).

Greater partnership and dialogue between adults and students and between students may offer a model of creative participation that overcomes some of the difficulties of other models. This is a whole school concern that may require a particular kind of school ethos. Here the necessity of dialogue, intergenerational understanding and mutuality are foregrounded. Working towards the democratic principles listed on pages 4–5 requires schools to work collectively and inclusively, to trust each other and recognise differences – even when this leads to disagreement.

Audience and youth participation

Creative practices (approaches and practitioners) may affect how youth participation and voice is conceived and mediated. They may enable a wider range of views to be sought and expressed, particularly in non-verbal or less formal ways that are less reliant on formal literacy. New forms of expression may require new ways of interpreting young people's voices and involve adults engaging in real dialogue with them.

Participation activities may happen some 'where', however this place is also connected with other places and spaces. Therefore it is important that young people (and adults) are provided with opportunities to take their new skills, resources and relations into arenas outside school. Evaluations of participation projects might then explore whether young people and adults are able to redeploy, rehearse and re-enact these new skills and resources in different contexts. This connects with the citizenship debate in considering how young people's participation in school may lead to wider action and connections with the local and global world around them.

Access and inclusion

Running through this book are ethical concerns about access and inclusion to youth participation activities. Practical concerns often mean that small groups of young people are chosen to take part in creative participation activities. It is important to consider the messages we are sending to young people when we make decisions, or set up processes to choose 'participating students'. The case studies that follow provide opportunities for you to think through the different messages, benefits and challenges in a variety of selection processes.

Who is this book for and how can you use it?

This book is for those who have an interest in promoting creative approaches to giving learners, teachers and other staff members, a say in schools. It is for those who are new to thinking about creative approaches to participation, as well as for those with some experience of it.

The book includes six case studies from schools in the UK who have developed participatory creative projects as part of the Creative Partnerships programme.[4] The case studies are diverse and include examples from secondary, primary and special schools, situated in rural and urban areas. They have been written by deputy heads, teachers, creative practitioners and young people who have been directly involved in these projects. The projects all took place in schools located in neighbourhoods where the majority of students experience social deprivation.

The authors all believe that young people have an individual and collective right to shape their education actively and that working with creative individuals and organisations, or adopting creative teaching and learning approaches, can support this aim. In doing so they challenge deficit views of young people and respect the knowledge, experience and capabilities that young people bring into school.

These case studies are not necessarily intended to provide specific lesson plans that can be taken on wholesale by schools but rather they offer an insight into what has worked (and not worked) in settings that may be similar to those that many of you work in. The voices, experiences and reflections of the writers help to form the 'story' of the work as they document what they did and why, what happened and what was achieved in the hope that you and other colleagues may be encouraged to try out such approaches yourselves.

As editor I have been privileged to work closely with the case study authors in shaping the chapters to ensure that they are readable and useful to others. The case studies are stories told by the teachers, young people and creative practitioners who were involved in the projects. I have offered questions and critical comments in the chapter texts where it seemed aspects of the story might facilitate and encourage deeper reflection and critical thinking – either by individuals or as a prompt for small group discussions. Professional development questions are provided at the end of each chapter that you may wish to explore with colleagues in departments or in whole school INSET sessions. Following the case chapters the appendix of the book offers some more detailed suggestions for how the case studies may be used to support professional development. Five staff development sessions are provided that can be used as they are or adapted for purpose. In the final section of the book you will find a variety of resources that may further support ongoing discussions and critical thinking in your own schools.

The book aims to encourage debate and discussion around the mutual roles of young people and adults in schools, sometimes challenging established and taken for granted practices and therefore requires reading with an open mind, ready to be inspired to share your thinking with others and develop creative ways of working with young people and other adults in your schools.

Chapter 2

This case study at Waverley School brings out the reciprocal roles of adults (teachers and creative practitioners) and young people as they work together in new ways. The authors highlight how creative interventions challenged static notions of teacher and student roles and raised the need for adults to understand youth to youth divisions and hierarchies.

Chapter 3

This chapter explores the process that led to Edgewick Community Primary School redesigning their curriculum and styles of teaching and learning. This whole school curriculum change involved intergenerational work and participation by both young people and teachers. This was a long-term journey for the school that involved challenging assumptions and identities and difficult moments but that ultimately led to the introduction of a new approach to learning and teaching in the school.

Chapter 4

In this chapter adults and children at Dunkirk Primary School co-produce their creative learning project. The co-production involved a three-way partnership between the teachers, the artist and the children in two classes. The authors point out that the existing ethos of the school helped to make this project successful. This ethos is described as one where adults were keen to be challenged and to challenge young people to debate and consider their own responsibilities to local and global environments.

Chapter 5

In this chapter Sally Cox describes young people's participation in important school decision making and INSETs. She discusses how the adults involved (including senior managers, governors and creative practitioners) were continually surprised by the young people and their capabilities.

The young people involved in this initiative developed their skills and resources further through work that they did with the local creative partnerships office and the local council – experiences that they bought back into their work as creative leaders in their own college.

Chapter 6

Ben Edwards from Three Ways School writes about a project which worked with young men who were marginalised from school life and describes how new ways of working enabled the boys and their teachers to take on new identities, both within the project space and within wider school practices. Ben describes the 'different' space created for the work through the use of multi-sensory teaching and learning techniques. He also suggests that participatory ways of working may change adult/teacher roles in schools through challenging traditional notions of roles and responsibilities.

Chapter 7

In this chapter Neil Small describes the benefits of a creative space (a Room 13) designed and run largely by young people attending West Rise School. Neil's description also suggests some of the challenges experienced where creative programmes are set up outside or independent of the usual practices and structures of schools.

Some critical questions

In this section you will find some critical questions that can be applied to aid the construction and practice of successful creative participation projects. As you read through the book it may be useful to consider the questions below as a starting point for thinking through the issues raised in this chapter:

■ *Who* is being asked to speak? Who is included? How do they come to be involved? How might this be viewed by others? What other ways of getting young people involved might there be?

- *What* are they being asked to speak *about*? What is the role of their prior knowledge, interests, experience, their lives outside as well as inside school, in this process?
- '*Who*' are they being asked to speak *as*? What identities are young people being offered in this process (examples might be: as citizens, activists, experts, learners, artists, audiences; as a collective, as special, gifted; as 'young', as male, female, black, white …)? How are they invited to see themselves? How might these identities relate to other identities they have, in and out of school? How are differences between and among young people taken into account?
- How is *creativity* defined? Is it a separate realm or everyday, and to whom does it 'belong'?
- *How* are they being asked to speak? What kind of 'voice' is enabled here? How might different approaches or technologies affect what is said?
- *Who* are they speaking *to*? Who is the audience? What relationships are established? What kinds of dialogue are enabled? What effect might this voice have?
- How *embedded* is this 'youth voice' in the daily practices of schools? And what might be the implications of this?
- What are the roles of *adults* in this process? Which adults are involved – and which are not? What differences and similarities are there between the roles of creative practitioners and teachers?
- How might this youth voice work be developed/improved? Why?

(Adapted from workshop materials by Bragg and Manchester, 2009)

Notes

1 The term 'creative practitioners' is used to indicate a range of arts-based expertise. Creative practitioners may include dancers, film-makers, installation artists, landscape artists, sculptors, musicians, painters, potters, storytellers and others.

2 Reggio Emilia is a philosophy of learning that promotes a creative and reflective approach to learning, with children at the centre. For more information see http://zerosei. comune.re.it/inter/index.htm, and http://www.latelier.org/index.php?option=com_ weblinks&view=category&id=2&Itemid=. In the UK http://www.sightlines-initiative. com/index.php?id=53.

3 A 'Forest School' is 'an innovative approach to outdoor learning and play' (see www. forestschools.com).

4 The Creative Partnerships programme brings creative workers such as artists, architects and scientists into schools to work with teachers to inspire young people and help them learn. (See http://www.creative-partnerships.com/.) The programme is delivered through locally based organisations who recruit 'creative agents' to work with schools to plan creative learning projects. Creative agents work closely with each school to appoint creative practitioners to deliver the projects, often alongside teachers, depending on the school's perceived needs.

References

Arnot, M. (2004) Working class masculinities, schooling and social justice: reconsidering the sociological significance of Paul Willis' *Learning to Labour*, in G. Dimitriades and N. Dolby (Eds.), *Learning to Labour in New Times*, New York: Routledge, 17–40.

Banaji, S., A. Burn and Buckingham, D. (2010) (2nd edn) *Rhetorics of Creativity: A Review of The Literature*. London: Creative Partnerships.

Bragg, S. (2010) (2nd en) *Consulting Young People: A Literature Review*. London: Creativity, Culture and Education.

Bragg, S., Manchester, H. and Faulkner, D. (2009) *Youth Voice in the Work of Creative Partnerships*. London: Creativity, Culture and Education. Available at http://oro.open.ac.uk/19371/

Craft, A. and Jeffrey, B. (2008) Creativity and performativity in teaching and learning: tensions, dilemmas, constraints, accommodations and synthesis. *British Educational Research Journal*, 34(5): 577–84.

Davies, L., C. Williams, *et al.* (2006) *Inspiring Schools: A Literature Review*. London: Carnegie Foundation.

DfES (2003) *Every Child Matters* (Green Paper). London: DfES.

Facer, K. (2008) What does it mean to be an 'adult' in an era of children's rights and learner voice? Futurelab Annual Conference: Why Learner Voice? University of Warwick.

Fielding, M. (2010) Patterns of partnership: student voice, intergenerational learning and democratic fellowship, in N. Mocker and J. Nias (eds) *Rethinking Educational Practice Through Reflexive Research: Essays in Honour of Susan Groundwater-Smith*. New York: Springer.

Fielding, M. and Bragg, S. (2003) *Students as Researchers: Making a Difference*. Cambridge: Pearson Publishing

Flutter, J. and Rudduck, J. (2004) *Consulting Pupils. What's in It For Schools?* London: RoutledgeFalmer.

Foucault, M. (1977) *Discipline and Punish: The Birth of the Prison*. London: Allen Lane.

Hart, R. (1992) *Children's Participation: From Tokenism to Citizenship*. Innocenti essays No. 4, Florence: UNICEF.

Jeffrey, B. and P. Woods (2005) *The Creative School: A Framework for Success, Quality and Effectiveness*. London: RoutledgeFalmer.

Masson, J. (2004) The legal context, in V. L. S. Fraser, S. Ding, M. Kellett, and C. Robinson *Doing Research with Children and Young People*. London: Sage, 43–58.

Morgan, B. (2007) Consulting pupils about classroom teaching and learning: policy, practice and response in one school. PhD thesis, University of Cambridge.

Osler, A. (ed.) (2000) *Citizenship and Democracy in Schools: Diversity, Identity, Equality*. Stoke on Trent: Trentham Books.

Osler, A. and Starkey, H. (2003) Learning for cosmopolitan citizenship: theoretical debates and young people's experiences. *Educational Review*, 55(3).

Rogers, C. (1970) *Encounter Groups*. London: The Penguin Press.

Rudduck, J. and Fielding, M. (2006) Student voice and the perils of popularity. *Educational Review*, 58(2): 145–57.

Thomson, P. (2007) Making it real: engaging students in active citizenship projects, in D. Thiessen and A. Cook-Sather (eds) *International Handbook of Student Experience in Elementary and Secondary School*. Dordrecht: Springer, 775–804.

Whitty, G. and Wisby, E. (2007) Whose voice? An exploration of the current policy interest in pupil involvement in school decision-making. *International Studies in Sociology of Education*, 17(3): 303–19.

Adult ambassadors and textile interventions
The birth of a creative youth panel

Sarah Joubert, Rachel Carter, Ruth Turnbull and Rehmuna Begum, Waverley School

Chapter overview

This case study describes how a secondary school in the West Midlands developed a creative 'youth panel'. The chapter explores the role of adult ambassadors in youth participation work, and the need to recognise this support. Adults are always involved in successful participation activities, perhaps providing access to skills, networks, and/or a range of material and cultural resources and facilities. In particular the case study explores the connected challenges of:

- increasing the power of student voices through involving them in decision making and working with staff;
- supporting staff to take notice and hear what young people have to say;
- recognising the effects of adult support, for example on who is asked to speak, about what, to whom.

Who's who?

- *Rachel Carter:* Creative agent, Waverley School
- *Sarah Joubert:* Advanced skills art teacher (AST),[1] Waverley School
- *Rehmuna Begum:* Pupil and youth panel member, Waverley School
- *Lisa Peterkin:* Head of specialism and assistant head, Waverley School
- *Ruth Turnbull:* Freelance textile artist

Sarah Joubert, Rachel Carter and Ruth Turnbull wrote this chapter collaboratively, with contributions from Rehmuna Begum. Sarah wrote sections that were concerned with school processes, Rachel wrote about the collaboration between adults and young people and Ruth wrote particularly about her own input to the project as a creative practitioner. They asked Rehmuna to comment on what they had written from a young person's perspective. In editing the chapter some of the distinct sections written by each contributor have been synthesised in new ways for the purpose of clarity; however a main author's name is attributed to each section.

The school context and key issues

Sarah Joubert

- *Name:* Waverley School
- *Location:* Small Heath, Birmingham
- *Age Range:* 11–16
- *No. on roll:* 780

Waverley School has seen rapid change and improvement over the last six years. We gained Specialist Humanities Status[2] in 2006 and began to work with Creative Partnerships in June 2008. It is an expanding school and at the time of writing was part of the Building Schools for the Future programme. It is due to become one of the first cross phase schools in the country.

At Waverley we value the diversity of the school community and respect the individuality of each person. We aim to foster an understanding of human values and attitudes, past and present and how society is organised, develops and changes. The school is very proud of our explorations of diversity, through termly 'diversity days'. However the school still faces many challenges as do many schools serving communities living in poverty. Challenges include responding to short-term policy goals, a high teacher turnover, teacher stress and a greater need than most schools for expenditure in relation to disciplinary and welfare issues.

Timeline

The development process

- *September 2008:* Bright Space (the local Creative Partnerships organisation) recruited three students from their five new secondary Change schools,[3] including Waverley, to join their Bright Space Youth Panel (BSYP).
- *November–December 2008:* A group of Year 7 and 8 pupils aged 11–13 (who had not been recruited to the BSYP) agreed to form a Waverley youth panel (WYP).

- *December 2008:* The word 'Aspirations' became the title for the first WYP project. The WYP participated in the process of recruiting an artist for the project
- *January–March 2009:* The Aspirations project took place

Editor's note

The word 'Aspirations' was chosen as the title of the project as 'it was a word that everyone understood and believed in,' (Rachel Carter, 2009) and because it also linked to the School Development Plan and current UK educational policies such as 'Every Child Matters.'[4] However, it may be worth taking a moment here to challenge the policy discourse in the UK. The assumption underlying the current policy emphasis is that 'aspirations' are too low, particularly among children from disadvantaged backgrounds and neighbourhoods, and that raising them is key to high achievement in education and the labour market as well as upward social mobility. Discourses around this term often suggest that aspirations (or a lack of them) are the result of individual shortcomings in young people or their families rather than structural disadvantage. In fact several recent academic studies[5] have found 'no evidence of any deficiency in terms of their motivation, aspirations nor willingness to work' and that young people of both genders, from deprived and non-deprived neighbourhoods and from different ethnic groups all have high educational and occupational aspirations.

Think about your own use of the term 'Aspirations' and the possible connotations of the word. Do you agree with the argument above?

Setting up the youth panel

Rachel Carter

As there was so much interest shown by young people in being part of the BSYP Rachel and Sarah thought it would be a good idea to set up a youth panel for Waverley School at the same time. This would be a small group of young people who would be trained to become spokespeople and event organisers to encourage creative approaches in the school. A group of around sixteen Year 7 and 8 pupils were invited to be part of this which was seen as a key tool in increasing student voice in the school.

Encouraging participation

We never presumed that the young people who joined the youth panel would have the confidence to express their thoughts, dreams and aspirations there and then, so we had to plan to set up a supportive and trusting environment for frank, open and honest conversations with the students. In order to ensure this the adults planned

Box 2.1   Ideas for ice-breakers

We started the meeting with two simple ice-breakers which got the students out of their chairs, laughing, having fun and also getting to know everyone's names and ensuring that they knew they were in a trusting, fun and creative environment:

1. A name game Mexican wave.
2. Lie game: each student to tell the group three things about themselves – one of them being a lie. The rest of the group had to work out which one was a lie.

Ground rules

This was followed by Rachel and the panel negotiating the ground rules for this Youth Panel. These were:

■ Everyone has something valid to say;
■ Respect each other;
■ Hear each other.

sessions carefully and included activities such as ice-breakers and negotiating ground rules (see Box 2.1).

The very first meeting sought student opinions when adults asked them what they liked and disliked about the school, what they might like to see more of, what they would like to be more involved in. Students identified that they felt the school needed to:

■ improve the school's termly diversity days;[6]
■ make lessons more fun and creative;
■ raise other people's aspirations and make Waverley a place that people wanted to come to.

Most of the Waverley Youth Panel (WYP) had much pride in their school and talked about wanting to communicate this to the wider community.

The adults observed and felt that involving the learners in this way and asking for their opinions from the outset of the project led to students feeling increased responsibility for and ownership of their own learning. It encouraged them to voice their own opinions, and work as a team from the beginning. However, this was not always a straightforward process as gender divisions were often at play between the young people in the group, as Rehmuna explains, 'At first it was all girls but then a few boys got involved but we sat separately. After a few meetings we grew fonder of each other and started to work together.'

Sarah and Rachel became aware of a huge change in the group dynamics during the project as students started to respect each other more and realised each student's importance within the WYP. They were using each other's strengths – with some pupils encouraging or pushing others to take particular roles within activities, for example more confidently spoken pupils introduced activities to primary school pupils, with quieter, less confident pupils using their creative skills to demonstrate textile techniques. As the project developed these roles started to merge as students started to support and encourage each other to try new things. Some pupils would become more nurturing and caring and helpful, others would become more organised when delivering activities to others. The pupils began to think of themselves in different ways in relation to other young people and adults in the school.

Recognition of divisions amongst students was important in building a cohesive youth panel at Waverley school. Can you recall a time when divisions amongst students have disrupted your own classroom or participation activities? What kind of adult support might help students to work together more effectively?

Involving students in decision making

Sarah and Rachel wanted the students to be involved in recruiting an artist to work with the youth panel. Representatives from the WYP were elected to take part in the various elements of the recruitment process. The whole of the WYP worked on the short-listing criteria and what they would look for in their artist when they gave a 'tendering workshop' as part of the recruitment process. Three members shortlisted the two artists from the many that applied. All the WYP took part in the two tendering workshops given by the shortlisted artists Ruth Turnbull and Frances Bossom, and three of them interviewed the artists.

After the workshops and interviews the students all wanted to employ Ruth Turnbull[7] because her workshop involved hands-on work making 'creatures' and all students felt proud of the work that they had created. Feedback from the students was that they also liked her friendly and relaxed approach to the workshop and working with the different textile materials. Sarah, Lisa and Rachel, however, wanted to employ Frances because it was evident from her workshop that she was committed to developing creative teaching and learning strategies with both staff and pupils. Her workshop was more process than product led.

Decision time: because Sarah, Lisa and Rachel are committed to listening to the young people and respecting their views and decisions Ruth was asked to come to work with the school. The students therefore felt that they 'owned' their project from the very start.

The adults here showed confidence in the young people's decision making, despite disagreeing with the decision made. Would you feel confident about doing this in your school? They describe the positive effects of trusting the young people. Can you identify any challenges or problems in adopting young people's decisions in this way?

Getting staff on board

Sarah Joubert

It was felt at this stage that it was also important to get staff on board and to let them know what was happening. We decided to involve the students as early as possible in every aspect of leadership, decision making and dissemination. As such it was extremely important to us and the students involved that it should be them who introduced new concepts and ideas to staff. Our staff are generally more passionate about our students than 'yet another school initiative' and we were passionate that they should not view our creative participation work in this way. Skilling our students to 'be heard' by staff at INSETs was a definite strategy; our staff listened harder and took ideas on board more quickly because our students were able to tell them what they wanted and why they wanted it. This set the creativity initiative in the school as one that engaged students as participants from the very beginning.

Therefore, at this early stage, Rachel and Sarah and three representatives from the WYP presented to the whole staff. The students were scared and nervous but they talked about their developing project, 'their artist', and their ideas for how they wanted to develop the WYP. Rachel and Sarah talked about Creative Partnerships and the aims of the Change school programme.[8] All the staff listened and were asked to come up with ideas for more creative projects in school. Feedback from staff to this presentation was great 'It's lovely to hear from our pupils', 'this was an interesting INSET!', 'Can we get more young people to lead INSET and workshops?'.

> Before the INSET we all felt excited and it was more like us jumping about everywhere and being nervous... just 2 minutes in I got scared, even though Ms Browster [now Joubert] was acting like a hero and going first. During the INSET my nerves were cracking because although I had done this before it was just that it was in front of so many people and they were teachers.
>
> (Rehmuna, Year 9 pupil and youth panel member, Waverley School)

Have you ever asked students to present their ideas at a staff INSET? What might be the challenges and benefits of such an approach? (Some are suggested above.)

Adult roles and relations

The adults bought with them a range of personal and professional skills, tools and experiences to the project. They believed that the project was such a success because of their shared vision and shared ownership. Throughout the project this shared vision was a strong link between the students, the teacher, the artist, and the creative agent and helped to develop a positive working relationship all round.

The adults involved in this project worked as a team with specific roles and responsibilities. While at Waverley Ruth found Sarah and Rachel to be extremely organised and approachable, they were both able to support Ruth before and during the project and nothing was too much trouble.

How might you go about assessing the impact of this kind of change in relations? What evidence might you look for?

Adult ambassadors of change

Rachel Carter

Sarah organised everything within school such as: timings, timetable, pupils, room, staff and school materials and was incredibly supportive of different events during the project. She supported pupils to continue working on some of the project ideas during extra days and was very flexible about letting them use her equipment, materials and other resources. She also acted as a 'broker' between staff and pupils through working with pupils to develop and present the project to other staff, and working hard and informally with both groups to challenge their expectations of each other. Sufficient energy and adept interpersonal skills were crucial in taking others who were less convinced on the same journey. Sarah's door was always open to staff and young people. She joined the school in Winter term 2008 at the beginning of the project but very quickly gained the respect and trust of most staff due to her openness, friendliness and commitment. An ambassador or champion who works in this way can be vital in young people's creative participation work.

However, such ambassadors also need the support of others. All those involved in the leadership and management of the project (Sarah, Rachel and Lisa) felt that in order to embed the changes that were happening it would be more effective to feed in gradually the ideas about creative teaching and learning and student involvement; proceed a few paces, allow staff to become accustomed and then develop the concept further. The same Vygotskian[9] 'scaffolded' or supported approach was taken with and by the students as they enticed more young people to come on their journey. Ultimately our management strategy became about making it easy for students and staff to get involved and become enthusiastic, then stepping back and allowing them to take ownership themselves.

Role of the creative practitioner

Sarah and Rachel trusted the creative process and were both very enthusiastic about the project. This allowed the pupils and Ruth freedom to explore the project creatively. There was time and flexibility for all participants to develop their ideas with no fixed idea of what the end of their 'journey' would be. The lack of pressure on the artist to support the creation of a final product meant that she felt she had more freedom to give young people time and 'space' to develop their ideas – creating a more equal partnership between adults and young people as they worked together.

Role of the creative agent

Rachel was always around and the pupils really enjoyed showing her their work. Having this support not only allowed Ruth to plan, deliver and evaluate workshops with confidence but also pushed the boundaries of the project and supported her to develop ideas to improve her own practice. Rachel also offered Ruth support in completing planning forms and evaluation documents, encouraging her to reflect in a form that felt appropriate for her (e.g. a sketch book) which Rachel then discussed with her for more formal project evaluation forms. She also worked to ensure that Sarah had the on-going support of a member of the senior management team so that the work could be influential across the school rather than in pockets.

Rehmuna comments on the adult support they received,

> We respected everyone and everything because we couldn't always have Mrs Joubert and Rachel with us. Some of our meetings didn't go so well when they weren't with us. Most of us treated these times like any normal meeting but some members took this as an opportunity to mess around, but then later on everyone participated and got properly involved as we had a job to do and we can't always rely on teachers – they have a life too!

Rehmuna here acknowledges the key role that adults played in the project. However her comments also suggest the difficult balancing act that adults need to manage when involved in projects that ask pupils to take the lead. How would you characterise this balancing act? What are the limits on pupils taking the lead?

The Aspirations project

Ruth Turnbull

At the beginning of the Aspirations project Ruth delivered a series of sessions working with the students to co-design and explore possible ideas and techniques for the project. In the first session Ruth handed out individual textile kits to each pupil which included a tape measure, a French dolly (for French knitting), an embroidery needle and a darning needle. Using their kit, each pupil made a needle case and learnt how to stitch a button of their choice onto the case. Pupils seemed to really like having their own kit and it gave them a sense of responsibility.

Ruth spent time showing pupils images of her own work such as using knitting to decorate trees and soft sculptures and also showed them other artists' work to inspire ideas. The pupils responded well to this and got really excited especially when they saw an image of a bus in China covered in knitting. The idea was that the pupils would be drawing on these examples to create their own textile installations and interventions in the school to encourage pupils to consider their aspirations and hopes for the future.

During explorations the students and Ruth decided to work towards a collection of temporary indoor and outdoor textile installations and creative interventions which would be situated around the school. WYP members here were positioned as anonymous artists who provided students and staff with an opportunity to 'have their say' by using craft to display messages and text around the school linked to the question around 'Aspirations'.

Ruth delivered textile based workshops where the students had the opportunity to investigate a range of textile and recycled materials while applying a variety of traditional and non-traditional techniques. These included: soft sculpture creatures, knitting with plastic bags, stitched padded objects, French knitted ropes, plastic bag pompoms and macramé. On two of the sessions pupils transformed spaces and objects (such as door handles, railings, trees, corridors) to make them stand out and seem more interesting and appealing as well as creating a fun element or talking point within the school.

The pupils also made their own recycled sketchbooks in which they were encouraged to reflect, using words and images, throughout the project.

Figure 2.1   Textile interventions in the reception area of the school

Figure 2.2 Student sketchbooks

Working with creative practitioners

Reflection on people and places in the school

Pupils were encouraged to reflect on the people and places within their school. For example, in one of the early sessions there was a group discussion about important people at Waverley school. The pupils thought that WYP pupils, Year 7 pupils, their head of house and parents were the most important and were clear that they didn't want staff or other pupils added to this list. They worked in pairs to make textile creatures to represent these people. The session finished with them evaluating the creatures and making speech bubbles to imagine what these creatures' aspirations were.

Pupils also took the artist on a tour of the school, finding spaces and places that they would like to decorate; they measured, photographed and recorded these findings in their sketchbooks. At the end of the session the pupils recorded their ideas, sketches and thoughts and reflections onto a large roll of wallpaper.

As the pupils reflected on their school environment and relationships with Ruth, school staff gained some unexpected insights into student worlds. Do you have the opportunity to do this in your own school? How often do your students have an opportunity to work with adults who are not teachers? What are the advantages of this?

Connections with cultural institutions and practices

Following the reflection and initial textile work in school the youth panel members were taken out of school to experience a gallery environment as an inspiration for their own work, and in order to contribute to their growing identities as 'artists'. The young people met the Education Assistant and other gallery staff at Walsall Art gallery. They were given a talk on the current exhibition and were allocated an artist's room to continue working and responding creatively to their project and to their experience at the gallery. The students loved this and were excited by the trip partly because they had so much to play with and reflect on at the gallery. This increased the young people's feeling of 'professionalism' and of being somehow 'special', valued and part of the school's working partnership to develop creativity across the curriculum.

Ruth encouraged the young people to feel valued and connected to cultural institutions and practices outside school. What kind of benefits might this bring to young people? What other resources might creative practitioners offer your students?

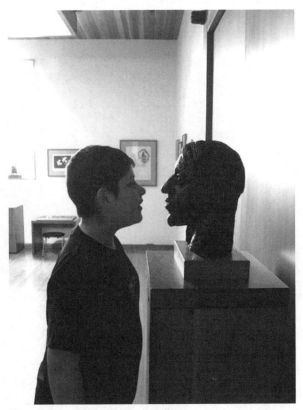

Figure 2.3   Trip to Walsall gallery

Contributing to other school initiatives

As part of the school's Diversity day the WYP delivered a very successful felt making workshops to sixteen younger pupils from a local primary school. In the workshop the WYP members developed their own ways of working and used their newly learnt textile skills to help and support the younger pupils. Working as creative learners gave them confidence, pride and motivation, allowing them to learn 'on the job' from their successes and mistakes.

There were some negatives, working in this project – we had to work with people we might not like, or were mixed up with people with or without a friend. We also had to be very organised and on time – which some of us were not very good at!

(Rehmuna)

Working with peers

Year 7 intervention activity

During the Aspirations project the pupils worked with Ruth to develop a Year 7 break time intervention where they showcased their practice, skills and professionalism. The WYP students produced a textile intervention and ran textile

Figure 2.4 A member of the WYP working with primary school children

activities to encourage other Waverley students and staff to use positive creative communication, and collaboration, while considering pupil and school aspirations. Ruth and the students set up an area in the main reception and installed some of the work they had been making such as textile creatures, macramé, French knitting and collage. This area is a main walk through during break-time so the WYP wanted to grab other students' attention and get them involved in the installation. The WYP chatted to students about their aspirations for the school and for themselves and encouraged these students to write these on tags and attach them onto the installation. The activity was originally only planned for Year 7 but there was an enthusiastic and thoughtful response from many pupils and staff, with so much positive and encouraging feedback and results. The WYP were gaining confidence and becoming very excited by the reaction. They wanted to continue and deliver the same activity to Year 8 and Year 9 pupils.

Working in this way helped the WYP students to realise other students' opinions, views and aspirations. It also helped them to understand the power that they have and how to use their creative ideas and techniques to engage large groups of people using art and craft as a tool.

> All the kids felt they were part of something special and for the first time we actually DID have a voice and more than seventy five percent of people who didn't recognise us back then are recognising us now and some people are asking us how they can join the youth panel and make a difference. Teachers also took notice.
>
> (Rehmuna)

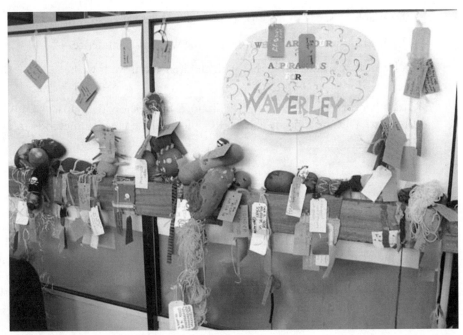

Figure 2.5 Year 7 intervention activity

As the young people grew in confidence they began to take the lead in developing creative initiatives in school. Are there any difficulties though in setting up a small group of students as 'creative leaders' in school? What messages might this send to other pupils?

Reflection and evaluation

The students and Ruth used the final session to evaluate and discuss possible ideas for the WYP to move forward and to develop ways of working with others. The WYP students showed that they wanted to pass on their learning to others and demonstrated that they had grown in confidence with ideas for organising charity events, working with the local community and running art/craft clubs for their peers. This project has given them a new outlook as to what is possible and how through working together they can achieve many things. They had some adventurous ideas: to organise a breakfast club for teachers, using pancakes and other breakfast food to relay messages to teachers about creative learning techniques; to set up a Graffiti Club to give graffiti artists in the school another outlet for their projects; to recruit new colleagues and to go on more trips, especially to art galleries and other cultural venues.

The young people involved in the project felt that they gained a lot, as they suggested in an end of project evaluation conducted by Rachel Carter:

> It was good that we were part of the WYP and getting a big say in everything.

> I was able to speak in front of a group of people.

> I got to know them, and that helped me with my confidence.

> I learnt how to work together with children and it went well.

What other sorts of evidence might you look for to show the impact of this kind of project? Who else might you ask? Could you use creative methods to assess impact?

What happened next?

A spin off from the Aspirations project was a transition project (the Equality project) funded by the school which allowed Ruth to continue to work with the WYP and Year 6 children from feeder primary schools to explore the meaning of equality while making textile creatures and habitats. The WYP were able to lead this project and continue to become more confident creative leaders while asking the younger pupils to think about equality.

The WYP

The WYP and Ruth are now working with teachers to develop a Creative Clinic, where the students will inspire staff to try some of the techniques developed and delivered in the Aspiration and Equality projects. This new project links directly to the school/staff vision of consulting pupils about their learning and giving them a say in how their lessons are delivered.

The focus for the Creative Clinic project is for young people to support teachers in the development of creative teaching and learning strategies and to further develop the school's skills-based themed curriculum. The Aspirations project helped them to develop the skills to be able to do this. The WYP students are leading the Creative Clinic project and are developing and exploring more creative ways of learning through exciting, fun and interactive textile activities. The pupils have already delivered a Creative Clinic CPD session to help teachers to become familiar with new craft and textile techniques and to discuss ways in which they could use these in their lessons. The pupils are decorating lab coats, gloves and badges and will be dressing up as Creative Doctors during the CPD session. The staff will hot-desk around the clinic workshops, picking up ideas, techniques and materials and a goodies bag (full of helpful resources and ready prepared activities to use in lessons). The project is allowing them to use craft as a tool for change and they are starting to realise how they can work as a team to influence their learning environment, using their creative ideas to enhance their learning experience.

Final reflections

Sarah Joubert and Rachel Carter

We are not doing everything perfectly and the constraints of the school building, lack of space and inflexibility of the timetable will continue to challenge us. But this is the beginning of a very long journey and we hope that we will work on the success of the Aspirations project and continue with our genuine shared vision to enable young people's creative participation in school life.

We believe that the success of the Aspirations project is related to the WYP being involved at every stage of the project, from advertising, to recruiting, to sharing, to reflecting, to management, to delivery.

The Aspirations project was all about the journey that the students and artist went on rather than the products that were made, as the project was focused on the students' voice both within the project and in their work with peers and other adults in the school. The skills learnt and product made enhanced the experience rather than being the centre of the project. The adults involved and the WYP enabled this through their shared desire for the students to lead the project, engage other pupils and develop a way of working that focused on process rather than on a final piece of art work.

In this way they were able to explore a more meaningful and sustainable way of working within the school and raise the profile of young people's voice in the school through challenging adult expectations about what young people were capable of.

Key learning and professional development questions

Adult–youth relations

In this project an effort was made to include teachers, and to change (some) teachers' perceptions about young people, from the very beginning. In this way the project saw adult–youth relations and intergenerational identities as integral to the participation project. This was achieved through challenging assumptions of capacity based on age through students delivering INSET and working closely with adults in choosing a creative practitioner and in making decisions about how the project would proceed.

Would you consider asking students to run an INSET in your school? Why or why not?

Youth–youth relations

This chapter suggests that it is important to consider (power) relationships between young people as they can often disrupt participation initiatives. Discuss whether this has ever been the case in your own practice? How might such projects work to de-stabilise identities that may be based on school practices (such as ability setting) and youth and other cultural practices? What kind of activities, methods, pedagogies and adult roles might achieve this?

The importance of adult support for young people's participation

This chapter suggests that youth participation work relies on adult support of various kinds, in providing access to skills, networks, and a range of material and cultural resources and facilities. Try to unpick the different roles that adult ambassadors and creative practitioners took on in this project. What factors led to their success?

Any youth participation activity therefore may also need to recognise and support those adults – acknowledging what they bring to the project. Consider how adults' own skills and expertise could be developed to support young people's creative participation through CPD opportunities or mentoring arrangements.

Now consider a more searching question that adults might ask themselves when working with young people in participatory projects.

How do you think this dependence on adult support might *generate*, *direct* and *shape* what young people feel they are able to speak about, how they might speak about it and to whom they might speak?

Notes

1 An AST is a teacher who has passed a national assessment and been appointed to an AST post. ASTs concentrate on sharing their skills, through outreach work, with teachers in their own and other schools.

2 The Specialist Schools Programme (SSP) helped schools, in partnership with private sector sponsors and supported by additional government funding, to establish distinctive identities through their chosen specialisms. Specialisms included: arts, business and enterprise, engineering, humanities, languages, mathematics and computing, music, science, sports and technology (see http://www.standards.dfes.gov.uk/specialistschools/).

3 Change schools work on a three year programme with Creative Partnerships. Artists and other creative professionals work across the school on a range of projects that involve exploring the creative potential of the pupils and the professional development of staff in the school (www.creativepartnerships.com).

4 Every Child Matters is a UK government programme that aims 'to improve outcomes for all children and young people' through joining up children's services.

5 See, for example, S. Sinclair, J.H. McKendrick and G. Scott (2010) Failing young people? Education and aspirations in a deprived community. *Education, Citizenship and Social Justice*, 5 (1): 5–20.

6 Diversity days were held once a term at Waverley. They were days when the whole school was 'off timetable' and activities were organised around a chosen country, e.g. Pakistan, Somalia.

7 www.ruthturnbull.com

8 Change schools work with Creative Partnerships on a three year programme designed to put creativity at the heart of the school's teaching practices.

9 A Vygotskian approach stresses the role of social interaction in learning and the need to 'scaffold' learning until learners become proficient to work on their own (L. Vygotsky (1978) *Mind in Society: The Development of Higher Psychological Processes*. London: Harvard University Press; J. Wertsch (1985) *Vygotsky and The Social Formation of Mind*. Cambridge, MA: Harvard University Press).

References

Bragg, S., Manchester, H. and Faulkner, D. (2009) *Youth Voice in the Work of Creative Partnerships*: Final project report. Newcastle: Creativity, Culture and Education.

James, A., and Prout, A., eds (1997) *Constructing and Reconstructing Childhood*. 2nd ed, London: Falmer Press.

Sinclair, S., McKendrick, J.H. and Scott, G. (2010) Failing young people? Education and aspirations in a deprived community. *Education, Citizenship and Social Justice*, 5 (1): 5–20.

Vygotsky, L. (1978) *Mind in Society: The Development of Higher Psychological Processes*. London: Harvard University Press.

Wertsch, J. (1985) *Vygotsky and The Social Formation of Mind*. Cambridge, MA: Harvard University Press.

3

Teacher-led creative participation

Designing a 'home grown' curriculum with young people

Debra Cleeland, Edgewick Community Primary School

Chapter overview

This chapter illustrates the importance of teacher voice in youth participation activities. The example from Edgewick Community Primary School, in the West Midlands, describes a journey that focuses on children's participation in their learning but also on developing teachers' professional competence, encouraging collaboration and reflective practice. This school did not work with a creative practitioner but rather was guided by one teacher who was inspired by ideas from creative professional development activities. In this chapter it is suggested that attending to 'teacher voice' is vital in enabling teachers to make profound (and potentially risky) changes to their pedagogy and relationships with students. The elements of their challenge can be characterised as:

- Building a curriculum that was cohesive and relevant to the children and their knowledge and experiences of the world;
- Developing teaching practices in the school to support such a curriculum.

Who's who?

- *Debra Cleeland:* Teacher and creativity co-ordinator, Edgewick Community Primary School
- *Pupil group:* Pupils who worked particularly closely with Debra from one class of children whom she taught for two years
- *Jayne McHale:* Headteacher, Edgewick Community Primary School
- *Helen Manchester:* Researcher, The Open University[1]

Debra Cleeland wrote this chapter with additional material provided by Helen Manchester based on her research work at Edgewick Primary School.

The school context and key issues

- *Name:* Edgewick Community Primary School
- *Location:* Edgewick, Coventry
- *Age range:* 3–11
- *No. on roll:* 250 pupils

Edgewick Community Primary School is located in the heart of a diverse community with almost all pupils coming from Asian and, increasingly, African backgrounds. The school is small with only eight teaching staff. There are over twenty languages spoken and the large majority of children enter the school at a very early stage of spoken English. The proportion of pupils with special educational needs and/or disabilities is higher than in most schools, as is the number eligible for free school meals. Transience is high, and the number of children who join the school partway through their primary school education is above average, though 'pupils who enter at other than the usual times, benefit from carefully planned support and soon feel part of the community' (Ofsted 2009 School Inspection Report).

The school's mission statement focuses on 'education for the community', 'celebrating diversity' and 'working together for success'. The headteacher is keen to work with the diversity of the children and the staff in the school and to 'make the most of everyone's talents'.

On entering the Creative Partnerships programme in 2006, the schools' priority was to find a more coherent and powerful way of developing young people's language and experiences effectively through creativity to:

- provide them with the skills and confidence needed to access and achieve within their curriculum;
- give increased context and relevance to their learning;
- provide a more equal platform for achievement.

We were also aware that to achieve the above, we would need to develop teaching practice in line with what our young people were indicating they needed to further and deepen their learning. This would require us to:

- develop teachers' understanding of different pedagogical approaches;
- strengthen teachers' confidence to enable dialogic teaching practice to take place;
- encourage teachers to move away from the traditional models of teaching they were used to;
- create a 'home grown' curriculum which profiled and addressed the personal and cultural needs of our learners;
- take the risk to co-construct a relevant and exciting whole new curriculum.

Timeline

This chapter describes a journey for the school, and the pupils and teachers over a three-year period. The practice starts small but the impetus quickly grows. The role of teachers in implementing change is crucial to this study.

- *Year 1:* Debra worked with her Year 4 class (aged 8–9 years) to change their classroom practices, exploring non traditional, creative learning and teaching styles. Senior managers in the school began to notice changes.
- *Year 2:* Debra continued to work with the same class. INSETs were held based upon and profiling the learning of pupils experiencing this dialogic learning process.
- *Year 3:* In direct collaboration with the young people, the school designed their own individual curriculum, which was non-QCA[2] based, whilst still ensuring curriculum coverage.

What did we do?

Debra here writes in the first person as she describes her own journey towards new classroom practices.

Year 1: One teacher and one class

I initially became interested in creative approaches through some Continuing Professional Development (CPD) organised by Creative Partnerships which helped me to question and develop the techniques I was using in the classroom. The training reaffirmed my belief that learning is about, 'exploring, investigating and expanding' and my vision of a creative classroom as one where dialogue, equality, discussion and collaboration are key elements.

Following the CPD, run by Mathilda Joubert,[3] and building on my own reading of philosophers such as Krishnamurti,[4] I was inspired to change my own classroom practices. The impetus for me was the opportunity:

- to be innovative and challenge the norm;
- to work in a more satisfying equality based relationship with young people;

- to demonstrate that deep learning is process not content based;
- to prove that there is more than one way to teach and more than one way to learn;
- to enable the whole class to take ownership of what we were doing.

Over a period of one year, I worked with the 8- and 9-year-olds in my class to record and evaluate the principles, practice and impact of: creative teaching, experiential learning, altered learner teacher relationships and the influence of the physical and emotional environment on learning.

This involved me working with my students to develop cross curricular approaches where there were no strict time segments for lessons. I moved away from a 'literacy' and 'numeracy' hour approach and instead worked with the children, judging pace according to their responses to learning stimuli. This involved ensuring there was time for children to consider and decide both *what* they learnt and *how*. This process was observed by the researcher:

> All the children are sitting in a circle in a space created in the room between the desks. Debra asks them to turn to the person next to them and discuss what they've been learning about in science and then feedback on what they've discussed. The children talk about many things that they've been doing that has excited them (and this is quite a lot) not making distinctions between subjects. They discuss their ideas and then Debra focuses in gradually on what they're going to be doing today and how it is connected with their previous work. Debra says that today they're going to be looking at what is a plant and what is not a plant. She asks the children to work in pairs again to come up with some ideas for what they think they might do/how they might work on this idea. As they talk in pairs Debra goes around the room encouraging them all to speak and requesting more noise. Looking around, all of the children are 'on task' and enjoying sharing their ideas with each other. Debra is continually praising them as she goes around the class.
>
> (Research fieldnotes, 2007, Helen Manchester)

Debra continues ...

I often used creative activities to inspire children to explore difficult or unusual concepts. For example, I would ask the children to use Lego, wooden blocks and CDs to make a model of something to express an idea, plan a story or answer an abstract question such as, 'Where do you think happiness lives?'

I also felt that through arranging the classroom and its fixtures in different ways children became more engaged. So I experimented with less sitting behind desks and more sitting in groups on the floor or in a whole class circle. I bought in cushions to make sure children were comfortable and happy to work in this way. I found that working in this way encouraged children to be honest and to talk about their feelings and experiences. We also spent less time working in exercise books and more time working on whiteboards, especially at the beginning of the year. This encouraged children to worry less about making mistakes or being messy and to concentrate more on content. I also made unusual changes to the classroom environment to stimulate discussion, for example putting displays upside down, or bringing in interesting resources from home and encouraging children to do this too. We did much more learning outside the classroom, making use of a log cabin and a wildlife garden in the school grounds.

One of the things that I felt was especially important was showing children that I valued their own cultures, lives and experiences. As we sat in a circle discussing learning I began to listen more carefully to what the children had to say. I found that children would talk about their interests and concerns, often in random ways that didn't at first seem to connect with what we were learning or talking about. However, by drawing on these comments and asking children to say more, for example about their favourite cartoon character, I found I could begin to change teacher–student relationships, becoming a learner as well as a teacher.

One of the other key changes I made was to introduce mixed ability learning groups into the classroom. Although there was some initial opposition to this from young people they gradually realised that this change benefited everyone. Learning in mixed ability groups challenged young people's own perceptions of their capabilities as well as their perceptions of other children's capabilities.

How far are current educational practices compatible with children's participation in mutual, collective learning? How would you feel about getting rid of ability groupings in your setting? What other aspects of your own classroom practices might you change to encourage more collaboration and mutual respect?

Years 2 and 3: Pupils taking the lead, designing a home grown curriculum

So, the work progressed in practical terms. In Debra's Year 4 class, learners' confidence, language skills and attainment were on the increase, and senior management were keen to filter what was being learnt and experienced through to the whole school. This class scored higher in standardised tests as well as demonstrating their confidence in conversation with adults and other young people in the school. The school was determined to build on and develop this strong partnership by involving these pupils in curriculum planning.

Regular INSETs were held based on participation and contribution, which were fun, active and experiential, and often pupil led. These were planned specifically to accentuate and profile the importance of flexibility, imagination, participation and ownership and an ethos of 'learning through mistakes'.

In these INSETs on-going and open discussions amongst staff and with pupils focused on these kinds of questions:

- What makes learning fun and most exciting?
- What environment best helps you to be the most imaginative?
- What are the best ways of encouraging creativity?

- What are the best ways of encouraging a group to work together?
- What can adults do to encourage dialogue and trust with young people?
- What are the benefits of consulting young people about their learning experiences?
- What are the best ways of creating an environment where everyone can succeed?
- Does creativity help learning?

Debra designed these questions with the young people in her class, as part of her on-going consultation process with them.

Do you feel that these questions are a useful starting point for discussions between teachers and young people in your setting? What might you add or take away from this list?

Initially, for some adults this process brought discomfort. For many, it meant dispelling inaccurate perceptions of what being creative was (i.e. 'arty'), and developing instead an understanding that thinking creatively is more about the ability to think independently, be innovative and solve problems. The lesson was that the most effective teachers are not only creative, but also encourage and facilitate creative learning[5] in their pupils.

Others though, welcomed this open, honest dialogue, which they knew instinctively would raise the level of their teaching and engagement of pupils in their class.

How do you understand the relationship between teaching creatively and creative learning?

The next section was written by Helen Manchester based on her research at Edgewick Primary School.

Following the work with young people, teachers also worked together on a process of change in a series of weekly staff meetings. In these meetings the whole staff examined their current practice in relation to their on-going discussions with young people. They identified as a staff the things they wanted to keep in their curriculum, and what they could do without. They then looked at the practicalities of how they could make this happen. The senior management team (SMT) were particularly committed to changing the school environment, the teaching and getting the children involved. Visitors from other schools were invited in to talk about their experiences of curriculum change and the headteacher visited a number of other schools. The whole staff then spent some weeks exploring models and 'thrashing out' what they felt would work in their context.

Implementation of the plans began in the next term. Staff were asked to provide evidence in their planning that they were considering a cross curricular or 'topic based' approach, and no longer slotting in 'subjects' to pre-defined curriculum time. Medium term planning would still include literacy and numeracy targets, however staff were also asked to produce weekly plans which clearly signposted how the curriculum would be delivered in a cross-curricular fashion and what changes they were planning to make to engage children as partners in their learning. The headteacher was aware that weekly plans should be flexible as 'it is what happens in the classroom that's important.' She therefore suggested that the weekly plans should show a 'direction of travel' but for teachers to think of their planning as 'fluid and ever changing, depending on the children's responses.'

The headteacher admitted that it is hard balancing this kind of curriculum change with the other demands made on schools. Particular challenges include, ever changing government agendas, and governmental organisations' continued reliance on 'basic stark data'. She admitted to being 'a bit outside my comfort zone because at the end of it we can't lose quality of the key bits, that's quite scary.' However she was committed to this curriculum change, partly because she felt that what they were doing before 'didn't focus on what seemed to matter.' She believed that working in this way would inevitably lead to 'deeper learning' and better results for their pupils.

The SMT were aware that this process of change would not be easy for some of their staff and therefore allocated time for them to prepare properly. For example, they arranged INSET days for teachers to work on re-organising their classrooms and preparing for each new half term. They hoped that this approach would bring about changes in the environment of the school that would help to stimulate learning and get children excited. In addition, enthusiastic and energetic ambassadors amongst the staff team modelled and disseminated outstanding creative practice, support mechanisms were put in place for those who needed them and teachers were encouraged to engage in on-going reflection and evaluation. With these approaches in place teachers began to demonstrate a willingness to move out of their comfort zones and develop more creative approaches.

The SMT also made time to talk frustrations over with staff both formally in whole staff meetings and informally with individuals. They tried to identify what was proving difficult and were proactive in trying to find solutions to these problems.

Although young people were included in the process of curriculum change, the SMT at Edgewick also felt it was important to provide spaces where teachers could discuss their own responses to young people's ideas and the integration of more creative approaches to curriculum delivery. What are the barriers to finding time for these kinds of teacher discussions? How could you find space for this in your setting?

Edgewick's 'home grown' approach: what did we learn from our young people?

Debra Cleeland

As staff worked together they also kept up their discussion with young people. Through on-going and open discussions amongst staff and with pupils' categories began to emerge. These were then grouped into headings that became the focus for the curriculum change in the school. These headings were communication and collaboration, resilience and risk taking, provocation/environment, flexibility, confidence, questions, evaluation, and momentum and change. Here Debra describes some of the implications for learning and teaching practices in the school.

Communication and collaboration

Our young people told us that they were more stimulated and engaged when they knew their voices and opinions were valued and an integral part of their learning experience.

As a school we agreed that this could be achieved through:

- facilitating discussion, reflection and dialogue throughout lessons to stimulate, engage, reinforce, challenge, consolidate and extend the children's ideas;
- including more group and partner work but also moving away from rigid ability groupings, thereby facilitating an environment which encourages children to pool together skills and resources and profile communication and collaboration as a powerful tool for deep learning, problem solving and creative thinking.

Through working collaboratively, cooperatively and honestly we began to see learning as a journey which is process led, strives to create something new and should not have a fixed outcome.

Resilience and risk taking

Together, we learnt that young people and adults need to collaborate to create a risk taking environment in which everyone feels secure to take risks and learns the confidence to express their opinions without fear, embarrassment and inhibition, therefore creating an environment that contributed to both emotional and intellectual growth.

We agreed that the best way to achieve this would be by:

- becoming overt equal partners in learning, modelling vulnerability and risk taking;
- striving to be innovative, inspiring and challenging;
- developing and embedding a consistent learning ethos which valued all contributions and embraced the unknown.

Indeed, our young people echoed research which showed that, 'the essence of creativity is in making new connections. These possibilities can be frustrated by rigid divisions in subject teaching which the current pressures tend to encourage' (NACCCE, 1999).[6]

Staff at Edgewick have begun to understand more clearly the interdependence of teachers and learners and how less hierarchical relations between teachers and learners can allow everyone to work outside curriculum boxes and take risks with pedagogy and learning. Can you identify practical ways that you could achieve this in your setting?

Provocation/environment

Our young people told us that a creative environment stimulates learning and places emphasis on questioning, thinking, believing and imagination. We learnt that by replacing existing classroom displays with less traditional ones (e.g. displays that showed the process of learning as well as an end product) young people could own and take charge of their learning more.

After reflection on what we were hearing, we planned to:

- continually experiment with and reflect upon our learning environments to facilitate our young people as natural investigators and to inspire imaginative thinking;
- arouse curiosity and learning through unusual objects, creative interventions and installations;
- provoke dialogue by challenging the features of a 'normal' learning environment to reinforce creative behaviours;
- continually stimulate new thinking and interest through the use of stimuli and experiential learning.

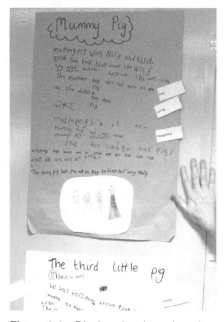

Figure 3.1 Display showing a learning process

Do you agree that the physical transformation of learning spaces can affect how children and teachers feel about learning? What practical challenges might making these kinds of changes present in your setting?

Flexibility

As adults worked together with young people (co-producing learning), we began to understand the need for a flexible approach to teaching and learning. For instance, this involved the ability to move fluidly between teacher and learner roles, and developing a more flexible approach to timetabling. A flexible and spontaneous approach actively supports diversity and therefore encourages innovative thinking and 'deep learning' to take place.

To facilitate the flexibility in learning that our young people valued and wanted, we planned:

- to challenge our personal perceptions and routines, to encompass alternative ways of doing things;
- to plan for purposeful not fixed outcomes, with plans demonstrating 'a direction of travel that is fluid and ever changing' (Headteacher, 2009);
- to facilitate teachers' as well as children's choices;
- to allow and plan for fluid movement from one group to another, without rigid labelling or preconceptions of ability;
- to create opportunities for learners to work together to plan and agree tasks and share responsibility for completing them.

The above points challenge rigidity in teacher planning and classroom groupings, aspects of which have become taken for granted practices in teaching and learning in the UK. What kind of changes would need to be made in your setting for these more 'flexible' approaches to be implemented?

Confidence/identity work

This new, 'dialogic' relation between pupil and teacher taught us that persistent encouragement, on-going emphasis on developing confidence, on diversity, perseverance, collaboration and modelled risk taking, are all powerful tools for challenging and changing identities and therefore often attainment.

To raise confidence, we planned:

- to challenge our own perceptions of ability (adults and children);
- to provide continuous opportunities for success through mixed ability collaboration, contribution and risk taking;
- to purposefully discourage low self-esteem by building the confidence and skills to make mistakes.

Debra describes 'challenging our own perceptions of ability' as a first step in turning around negative learning identities. How might you go about doing this?

Open and philosophical questioning

Our young people told us that open/philosophical questions broadened their thinking and helped them develop skills which promoted learning at its deepest level. We discovered that these questions can be used to nurture a learning environment in which pupils learn that asking questions and hypothesising is a good thing and that we will not always know the answer. We also discovered that open questions promoted diversity in answers and created a more equal platform for discussion.

We planned to increasingly use open/philosophical questions as a stimulus for dialogue, exploration and meaningful learning. Examples of such questions include:

- What is the meaning of life?
- Are all people born good?
- What is the meaning of love/truth?
- Why do we have to get up in the mornings?

Images were also used as prompts for discussion around questions such as:

- What do you think the person is thinking?
- Do you think you would get on with them?
- What do you think they'd think of you?
- What do you think they're really good at?

Take a topic from your own curriculum and consider how you might use more open/philosophical questions in order to extend pupils' learning.

We have distilled out practice and our learning from this project into the following checklist of practical advice:

- Only ask questions (e.g. what makes your learning fun/difficult) if you are prepared to listen and act upon what you hear. Don't pay lip service to student ideas.
- Keep a clear vision.
- Set the tone – explain that you are interested in what your young people have to say because you believe that it will ultimately benefit the whole school.
- Demonstrate a commitment to those people you are consulting with by sharing some of your plans with them.
- Have a 'no repercussions' policy about what is said.
- Do lots of ground work ensuring that all parties have a shared understanding of what is being asked, i.e. 'what does it mean to be creative/have increased ownership?'

- Think carefully and strategically about who your ambassadors will be.
- Be encouraging, supportive and patient.
- Encourage a non-confrontational and non-critical approach.
- Don't expect everything to happen overnight.

Professional development questions

Teacher voice

The headteacher in this school believes strongly that teachers' voice is important in enabling student participation throughout school, and in fact that in this school the teachers required opportunities to build their confidences and understandings in order to develop student participation. As she explained:

> ... it's not just about the children because if the teacher's not happy and excited about what they're doing then they're not going to make much of an impact on the children.

Think about student participation activities happening in your school. What are the implications of this for your own activities? Write a list of the approaches you could take to ensure that teacher voice is also given prominence in any 'youth' voice activity.

Really listening to children?

Debra and her colleagues ask young people for advice on how the school might make learning more relevant to them. What are the challenges in adopting this kind of approach with young people?

How might you use children's ideas as a starting point for a dialogue with young people, rather than feeling that what they say must be listened to and embraced without critique?

Definitions of creativity

Debra suggests that some teachers feel that they need to be 'arty' in order to develop creative approaches. It can be hard to pin down the notion of creativity – this has led some schools to work together to define their own version of creativity, appropriate to their context.

How might you go about doing this in your school?

Discourses of creativity[7]

Likewise, some of the discourses around creativity may need unpicking in relation to your own context.

How do you feel about the use of words such as 'resilience' and 'risk taking' in this chapter? What do they mean in your context?

Notes

1 I spent time in Debra's class as part of my role as a researcher on the research project funded by Creative Partnerships, 'Youth voice in the work of Creative Partnerships' (2007–2009).

2 QCA: Qualifications and Curriculum Authority in the UK (governmental organisation at the time).

3 Mathilda Joubert is a consultant, researcher and trainer in creativity, innovation, organisational development and the management of change. She works nationally and internationally with organisations from across the business, arts, education and voluntary sectors (http://www.softnotes.com/index.php).

4 J. Krishnamurti (1981) *Education and the Significance of Life*. London: Harperone.

5 See B. Jeffrey and A. Craft. (2004) Teaching creatively and teaching for creativity: distinctions and relationships. *Educational Studies*, 30 (1): 77–87.

6 'All our Futures' (1999) was a report made to government by a committee led by Ken Robinson on the creative and cultural development of young people through formal and informal education: to take stock of current provision and to make proposals for principles, policies and practice. Downloadable at www.cypni.org.uk/downloads/allourfutures.pdf.

7 See S. Banaji and A. Burn (2010) *The Rhetorics of Creativity: A Review of The Literature*. London: Creative Partnerships.

Students as creative consultants

Researching and developing a new pastoral system

Sally Cox, Guthlaxton College

Chapter overview

This chapter documents how a small group of young people were placed in positions of governance, and the effects of this on a school. In this example, from Guthlaxton College, in the East Midlands, teachers and creative practitioners provided the young people with quite extensive training which was seen as necessary for them to fulfil their role effectively. As a consequence of the project, adult expectations of what young people were capable of increased as the young people engaged in decision making about key processes in school life. Challenging adult perceptions of young people may be an important way in which creative approaches can contribute to a school culture. The elements of the school's challenge can be characterised as:

- the need to develop students as independent learners;
- the pressure to personalise learner experiences and maximise their potential in every aspect of their life at college in a very large institution (each year cohort contained over 500 students);
- meeting the demands of an extensive examination orientated curriculum;
- understanding and working with students who were making a transition to a new school (at 14 years old) whilst also coming to terms with the physical and hormonal changes of adolescence, preparing for adulthood with many facing crisis in their home life.

Who's who?

- *Sally Cox:* Deputy principal, Guthlaxton College
- *Deborah Wilson* and *Natasha Davies:* Assistant principals, Guthlaxton College
- *Mathilda Joubert* (softnotes.com): Independent consultant, creative thinking and youth participation work
- *Di Goldsmith:* Creative agent, Guthlaxton College
- *The creative consultants:* Twelve Guthlaxton College students selected from Key Stages 4 and 5 (aged 14–16)
- *Peter Osgood:* Governor for performing arts, Guthlaxton College

Sally Cox wrote this chapter with contributions from Mathilda Joubert and Helen Manchester. Mathilda and Helen's contributions are clearly indicated in the text.

The school context and key issues

Guthlaxton College is a Leicestershire upper school catering for young people aged 14–19 years old. Guthlaxton College has a truly comprehensive intake. Our current students in Years 10 and 11 (ages 14–16) are statistically some of the most deprived of all Leicestershire upper schools.

There is a strong tradition of student participation in decision making across the college including house councils, the sixth form management committee and the whole college student council.[1] Students have been involved in contributing towards significant decisions such as the appointment of staff including senior managers, the introduction of new catering arrangements and the development of a virtual learning environment (VLE).

In this chapter we discuss 'Shift Happens' – the creative programme for change at the college in which teachers were challenged to implement new practices in learning and students were offered the opportunity to develop independent learning styles through increased participation in decision making and governance.

Timeline

- *September–November 2008:* Planning and development activities
- *November 2008:* Creative consultants nominated and appointed and training begins
- *December 2008:* Inaugural meeting and in house training with the deputy principal
- *January 2009:* Student-led research gathering and creative practitioner INSETs
- *Mar 2009:* Student feedback to governors, student body and teachers
- *Apr 2009:* Wider consultation
- *May/June 2009:* Decision making
- *September 2009:* Creativity day

Box 4.1   The young consultant programme (Helen Manchester)

The creative consultant programme running in this school is part of Creative Partnerships (CP) Leicestershire/East Midlands (known as 'The Mighty Creatives') response to raising the profile of young people's participation. Each CP school in this area is required to appoint a small team of students, called the creative consultants. According to Richard Clark, the area director, these students should then be trained up with a focus on 'the professional development of those young people as partners in their creative partnership'. The aim is to mature and develop the young people's experiences over a sustained period of time.

The young consultants (YCs) are involved in regular conversations with creative agents and practitioners, as well as with teachers. They are given opportunities to participate in events and training outside school. They have also been recruited to work as consultants by the local council and other bodies interested in young people's views.

It is hoped that existing YCs will support the training and development of others through 'mentoring, coaching, acting as champions for the work'; and new YCs will work on a rotational basis, spending one year learning about the role, a second year developing their expertise and a third year training new recruits.

Planning and development activities

The academic year began with the student council inviting the student body to comment upon their needs and the factors which were 'enabling' and 'barriers' to their learning. Students suggested a number of enablers and blockers including the number of students attending the college, fear of the future, no quiet space at home to study, ridicule by peers, subject knowledge of teachers, use of ICT and so on. By far the most important barriers to student learning identified in this consultation were the size and pastoral structure of the college.

A joint action group was established to explore the issues raised by the student body. This group included students, teaching and associate staff and governors and was initially led by two assistant arincipals. The list of enablers and blockers to learning were explored and shared across a range of stakeholders. The stakeholders in the action group considered these findings and asked a newly established group of twelve students called the 'creative consultants' to work with their teachers to investigate and devise some creative solutions.

The creative consultants

The creative consultants (aka 'young consultants') at Guthlaxton College were a group of twelve students nominated by their group tutors and subject teachers. These students formally applied for the position and were short listed and interviewed by a panel of students and staff. This led to the creation of a group of motivated and ambitious young people. The creative consultants initially received a range of training opportunities (discussed further below) with creative practitioners, the college's creative agent and the CP delivery office. The consultants were involved in visiting local theatres and acting as critics of practitioners, developing briefs for conferences, interviewing for key positions and working on internships at the regional CP offices. Through participating in these opportunities outside school the creative consultants developed expertise and grew in confidence, particularly when working with adults.

> What kind of young person would you expect to be recruited through these sorts of processes? What kind of concerns might this raise in relation to issues of access and inclusion?

The role of the creative practitioner: training and INSETs

Mathilda Joubert

I worked first with the team of creative consultants to explore the nature of creativity and how it can be enabled across the curriculum. The discussions were based on my own definition of creativity: 'Creativity is the application of independent original thinking.' The creative consultants explored different aspects of this definition in participative and practical ways. For instance they explored the notion that creativity is not necessarily the arts, but a thinking process that could be applied across all subject areas, that creativity involves original and purposeful thinking and that young people are well placed to encourage their peers to develop new ideas, rather than needing teachers to always do this for them. They also explored the difference between the concepts of 'teaching creatively' and 'teaching for creativity' that were outlined in the 1999 NACCCE report,[2] recognising that the key difference lies in who does the original thinking in the lesson: the teacher or the students? The creative consultants then generated a list of classroom activities that they thought could lead to greater 'teaching for creativity' in lessons. This list included:

- decision making exercises
- investigation work
- expression opportunities
- improvisation
- debates and group discussions
- teacher–pupil interaction
- freedom to think (getting on with it)
- spontaneity and difference valued
- changes in environment to stimulate thinking
- 40 per cent teacher, 60 per cent student led activity as an ideal balance in lessons

The session with the creative consultants was followed up by a whole staff INSET on creative teaching and learning in which the team of creative consultants participated. The session with staff also focused on exploring *what* creativity is, *why* it is important for young people to develop creative thinking skills and on *how* to enable it across the curriculum. Staff considered how creativity in the curriculum can be influenced by where we teach (the learning environment), what we teach (the curriculum) and how we teach (the pedagogy or teaching style). The same definition of creativity and differentiation between teaching creatively and teaching for creativity was used as the basis of this interactive training session.

The creative consultants interacted incredibly well with staff in the training session, joining different teacher teams for different activities. The presence of the young people contributed to a very positive atmosphere in the room and created the expectation for staff to engage fully with the training activities, rather than sit back and switch off. I think it was also really powerful to add some of the young people's ideas for increased 'teaching for creativity' into the training session. In-depth discussions were held about their points, particularly concerning the ideal ratio between teacher-led and student-led activity in class. Student participation in these sessions began to challenge established divides between adults and young people in the college.

This whole staff INSET was followed up with more extensive INSET sessions for the large and active teaching and learning team across the college on the Personal Learning and Thinking Skills (PLTS) model and social and emotional aspects of learning (SEAL). The INSET was not run in a prescriptive way but encouraged participation and reflection, focusing on how these initiatives could be integrated into their teaching and learning. I asked teachers to try out new approaches in an experiential way, rather than simply talking about them. In this way they were able to adapt the ideas as appropriate to purpose, context and subject area.

> Mathilda describes her approach to INSET delivery. What do you think creative practitioners like Mathilda bring to this process that is different and valuable? How does this relate to young people's participation?

Student researchers

Through this interaction with staff and the creative practitioner the creative consultants developed their expertise and thinking in relation to creativity and gained credibility amongst staff. In addition to the creative practitioner training some intensive in-house development work was also seen as necessary to enable the creative consultants to participate in school decision making. Therefore over a period of eight weeks the creative consultants met twice weekly with one of the deputy principals to debate policies and procedures, such as college dress, punctuality, work experience, the use of the college campus. These meetings challenged the students to learn independently and to use the resources around them to research these issues in preparation for a deep-seated debate. The deputy principal gave the students enough space to explore ideas critically, whilst also being clear that she valued their opinions. The investment of time by both the students and the member of staff was enormous as was the level of trust given to the students by the deputy principal. However, the risk was well worth taking, in the words of the consultants 'we were set free to explore creatively with no constraints.'

What kind of risks do you think that the deputy principal is talking about here? Consider the starting point for and the focus of the student participation work. Why was so much training required in this case?

The initiative and enthusiasm of four key consultants provided a positive leadership role model. The students took ownership of the problem and embarked upon a programme of research using the Internet as their tool to investigate pastoral structures of other schools and colleges. Guided by the two assistant principals a core group of eight students made contact with a number of institutions and arranged visits to explore alternative pastoral models.

This kind of research is often conducted by adults. What might be the benefits of asking students to do this work? What are the challenges?

The creative consultants used the school's Virtual Learning Environment (VLE)[3] as a tool to gather questions from fellow students to inform their visits to other schools. They visited tutor groups with questionnaires and made presentations in year groups. The students were highly inventive using the plasma screens around the college to focus interest, the college website and designing post boxes to elicit student ideas on a postcard. The students adopted a high profile in assemblies, at lunch and break times and were determined to involve as wide a cross-section of the student body as they could.

Following their own research and training the creative consultants visited other schools armed with questions suggested by their contemporaries. A group of teachers (who also had questions) visited with them and in this way the evidence gathering process took place. Again students and teachers worked together in new ways and on an equal footing as they explored their complementary but different concerns and questions.

On return to school the students gave feedback and presentations to the staff and to the student council. The process of student research was supported by the principal who offered a lunch time opportunity for students to ask him questions. This sent a clear message to the students that they were being listened to and taken seriously within the school.

There was a great debate amongst all stakeholders, particularly at action group meetings. Importantly at these meetings the chair was rotated amongst members, giving student members an equitable share in taking on this role. The students had gathered information and ideas from their visits, and with the teachers and governors on the action group were able to formulate some alternative suggestions to remodel the structure of the college. These models were shared with stakeholders at governors and staff meetings and with students in morning assemblies and through the use of the VLE.

There was some resistance to change from a core group of staff, students and governors who felt, for example, that 16–18-year-old pupils in the school should form separate tutor groups. Further visits to schools and colleges which had successfully made the transition to vertical tutor groups were made and through dint of student persuasion tough arguments were won. It was at this point that governors and staff acknowledged the credibility of the student voice which proved the turning point of the process.

What seem to be the benefits of working with a small team of students for a sustained period of time and providing them with special training? Are there any disadvantages in such an approach?

Engaging peers

The creative consultants developed a 'room' on the VLE to gather opinions concerning their models for restructuring the school. Their ideas were formed and reformed as opinions swayed from one model to another. Group tutors used the VLE during personal development time to engage students in the debate and it was used in core IT lessons as a stimulus to engage students in the debate. There was a 10 per cent response from individual students (152) and an 86 per cent response from fifty-four tutor groups. The most popular model which emerged was the vertical tutor group system across houses. However the heated debate centred upon whether it should be whole college, that is 14–19, or two separate cohorts 14–16 and 17–19.

The core group of consultants worked relentlessly to engage their peers in various forums including a lunchtime surgery with the principal and other senior staff. They were supported by the two assistant principals. Tutor groups were visited and presentations made; a presentation was made in assembly and again the plasma screens – places in student populated areas and the college website were used to communicate the process.

The students here used various forms and technologies to consult with fellow students and in this way perhaps engaged a more diverse cross section of the student body. What other methods and approaches might enable more inclusive approaches to whole school consultation?

Students as active participants: 'creativity' day

Through their wider involvement in the 'Creative Partnerships young consultant programme' the creative consultants attended staff training days and twilight sessions, participated in interviewing for key positions at the Mighty Creatives (TMC) (the local Creative Partnership organisation) and organised a Mighty Creatives conference for 200 pupils. This engagement in activities outside the college setting was important as it provided them with opportunities to practise their new found confidence and skills beyond the college setting. As a result of their experiences they also recognised the need to develop a more creative approach at the college to embed the new pastoral system.

At an action group meeting they forwarded the recommendation that for vertical tutor groups to work successfully the students and teachers needed to be provided with an opportunity to bond and to get to know each other. Their suggestion was a collapsed curriculum day with creativity being the driver to break down barriers, support relationship building and enhance learning. This idea evolved from the practice of collapsed curriculum days in their Key Stage 3 High Schools (ages 11–14) where the usual curriculum is ignored for the day and other activities arranged for students instead. They also drew on their own training and experiences discussing and participating in creative approaches with creative practitioners in school and within the CP young consultants programme.

The creative consultants worked closely with the link governor for Performing Arts in planning the day – a new role for governors at the college. The commitment and enthusiasm of the students for the programme and the previous role the governor held as a Local Authority Arts Co-ordinator added to the success of this partnership. The governor stated that she was amazed by the understanding, knowledge and confidence of the students. An advertisement was placed for creative practitioners to be involved in the delivery of this collapsed curriculum day and to work with tutors and students to embed the new ethos and support learning. This initiative was planned, delivered and evaluated by four of the consultants who alongside the governor interviewed over eighty-five creative practitioners. They set the criteria, wrote the interview questions and debriefed the unsuccessful applicants. They appointed twenty-five practitioners who worked with students and their tutors in September to embed the new pastoral structure.

As the day approached the creative consultants organised the programme and liaised with the heads of house and local high schools for alternative venues. They commissioned a group of drama students to present the idea in assembly and they recruited helpers to assist them. In addition, they were trained by our creative agent[4] to act as evaluators for the day seeking evidence of the impact. They designed an evaluation that included observations of and interviews with the students, looking at their engagement in the work, post activity comments and recordings and an evaluative questionnaire completed by staff and students. On the day they met and greeted and acted as hosts ensuring careful co-ordination and a successful outcome of the activity. The students designed the tasks and communicated this to the creative practitioners and group tutors. It was evident from the feedback that students, tutors and creative practitioners had learnt from the experience.

The role of creative practitioners

The value of the creative practitioners as catalysts for bringing together the tutor groups was key to the success of the day which gave rise to 'a genuinely diverse input' (creative practitioner). One group tutor stated that the creative practitioners brought 'skills and talents in creativity and were so willing to share and get stuck in.' Creative practitioners had no written brief or prior planning for the event and were asked to work in partnership with tutor groups to plan the day and create artefacts such as mascots, logos and presentations. The practitioners here modelled a new kind of (more flexible) approach for many tutors. In addition, one tutor suggested that the creative practitioner was able to create a positive affective space because of his own lack of inhibitions: 'unlike me, he had no inhibitions and was able to stretch the tutor group in such a way that it broke down all the barriers and hang ups across the year groups.'

Utilising the experience and creativity of total strangers, who were sword fighters, dancers, jugglers, poets, DJs, cheerleaders and so on, enhanced the quality of the opportunity and demonstrated the value of vertical tutor groups. In the words of a student 'you don't have to know others to get on with them and learn from them, even strangers in a short time can be a part of the team so there should be no bars to us getting on'.

Sally suggests that the creative practitioners brought something additional to the day that helped to create a space for dialogue between young people of different ages. What does this additionality seem to include?

Key learning

Challenging adults' beliefs about what young people are capable of

The creative consultants demonstrated to college staff, governors and their contemporaries that they had leadership and management skills. This was arguably only possible because they were given credibility to initiate, develop and evaluate the project themselves and because of the role played by adults in fostering and nurturing the young people as individuals and as team members. The governors were astonished by the attitude and approach of the creative consultants despite being initially reticent to allow them the independence to explore the task and champion vertical tutor groups. Equally, teachers and associate staff were sceptical of the extent to which the consultants could act as 'movers and shakers' upon such a key issue of the day to day operation of college life. The partnership which evolved within the action group was an equitable relationship of governors, teachers and associate staff and students who quickly realised that the creative consultants had powerful and totally valid views and opinions.

This initiative has clearly raised adult expectations of what young people are capable of in this college, in particular their ability to engage in research and decision making processes.

Consider the expectations of young people in your school. Do you feel that staff generally have appropriate expectations of young people's capacity to be involved in making key decisions about school life in this way?

Opportunities for personal development and learning

The creative consultants became leaders of change taking on a role as 'co-producers' of learning across the college. This process offered opportunities for confidence building, raising self-esteem and establishing and maintaining positive relationships. These relationships developed over time and the consultants have stated that it has been great to work with other students of like minds, i.e. drive, ambition, energy and vision.

The young people became independent thinkers, taking increased responsibility and sharing a willingness to lead through chairing meetings, writing and administering questionnaires, setting up interviews with creative practitioners and so on. The learning curve was immense and offered opportunities for development in speaking and listening, patience, determination, and the need to be resolute and show rigour.

Skills were gained and opportunities experienced which had not been recognised as outcomes from the work. One student commented that, 'I was able to gain confidence and to develop individual skills and talents in decision making and what was more, use these to maximum effect.' The students gained credibility and ownership of the initiative and they emerged from the process leading through advocacy.

What happened next?

The work continues and incredibly the momentum has been sustained. The creative consultants have recruited new blood through a campaign and an interview process. They are now mentoring this new cohort of creative consultants.

They have led an area conference for the pupil councils in the borough of Oadby and Wigston (October 2009); introduced and developed the house captain initiative and house councils (October 2009); they have reshaped Guthlaxton for the future through working with an architect to introduce and develop new building designs (Autumn 2009) and are initiating and developing the Year 2 programme of the Change School. This has involved forging links with the Curve Theatre in Leicester to design and deliver a week long residency for twenty-five Year 10 vulnerable students. The purpose of the opportunity is to explore the

Box 4.2   Flutter and Rudduck's student researcher model

4 Pupils as fully active participants and co-researchers
Pupils and teachers jointly initiate enquiry, pupils play an active role in decision making along with teachers, and they plan action in the light of data and review the impact of the intervention.

3 Pupils as researchers
Pupils are involved in enquiry and have an active role in decision making; there will be feedback and discussion with the pupils regarding findings drawn from the data.

2 Pupils as active participants
Teachers initiate enquiry and interpret the data. Pupils are taking some role in the decision making; there is likely to be some feedback to pupils on the findings drawn from the data.

1 Listening to pupils
Pupils are a source of data; teachers respond to the data but pupils are not involved in the discussion of findings; there will be no feedback to pupils, teachers act on data.

0 Pupils are not consulted
There is no element of participation or consultation.

concept of the independent learner, bringing to the college a 'teaser campaign' and an 'installation concept' as an opportunity for all learners to explore, develop and foster their own learning styles. This project is called the 'Learning Curve' and provides an excellent progression from 'Shift Happens'. It is an exciting project which once again indicates that the creative consultants are able and willing to work in partnership with adults to build innovative learning projects.

The success of 'Shift Happens' secured a new role for students at the college which will be both a legacy and a catalyst for on-going advocacy and governance by students at Guthlaxton College.

Professional development questions

Consulting young people about teaching and learning

1. Look at the model proposed by Flutter and Rudduck (2004) in Box 4.2. Which models were adopted in this project? Were different models adopted at different stages of the project? From your perspective as a teacher/ senior manager what are the advantages and disadvantages of the different approaches?
2. Consider the different modes of consultation used by the students. How might each of these play a role in generating, directing and shaping agendas; what can be spoken about, how and to whom?

Access and inclusion

The young consultant programme recruits cadres of young people to take on roles in school in relation to creative learning and approaches in school. By their very nature such initiatives involve only small numbers of students at any one time.

They may serve an important public and symbolic purpose for a school as evidence of its commitment to youth participation. However, it may be important to also consider:

- how young people are recruited to these groups and the impact of this on issues concerning access and inclusion;
- how their work, and the processes by which students come to be part of them, are perceived by peers, and how they might gain credibility amongst both students and staff;
- how they can evolve, develop, share skills and reach across different groupings within a school.

Notes

1   *House council:* the College has four houses each of which has a council made up of representatives of the student body.
    Sixth form management committee: this is a team of students including the head boy/girl and deputy head boy/girl who work with the sixth form leadership team to manage the sixth form social affairs.
    College council: this is made up of student representatives from the House Councils and Sixth Form Management representing the view points of the student body.
2   'All our Futures' was a report made to government by a committee led by Ken Robinson on the creative and cultural development of young people through formal and informal education: to take stock of current provision and to make proposals for principles, policies and practice. Downloadable at www.cypni.org.uk/downloads/allourfutures.pdf
3   The VLE is an online tool used across the college as a tool for learning and is often accessed throughout and beyond the college day with all students being able to access it at home.
4   A 'creative agent' is a creative practitioner who is experienced in working in educational settings in an advisory and enabling capacity.

References

Flutter, J. and Rudduck, J. (2004) *Consulting Pupils. What's in It For Schools?* London: RoutledgeFalmer.

National Advisory Committee for Creative and Cultural Education (NACCCE, 1999) *All Our Futures: Creativity, Culture, Education*, May 1999.

5

Small actions – big change
Co-producing creative approaches in school and out

Claire Simpson, Asima Qureshi and Parmjit Sagoo, Dunkirk Primary School

Chapter overview

This chapter describes a project in which young people's participation was integral to the curriculum and ethos in the school and involved them working in partnership with adults and with each other in 'co-producing' learning. Dunkirk Primary School, in the East Midlands, has worked closely with artists for six years. The project described in this chapter involved two whole classes in the school – Year 1 (5–6-year-olds) and Year 2 (6–7-year-olds) and explored global environmental issues. The two classes worked with a creative practitioner and their teacher for half a day each week but many elements of the project were developed in core curriculum activities in class.

The elements of their challenge can be characterised as:

- the pressure to improve attainment in all subjects, particularly literacy;
- the need to ensure all children were motivated, engaged and challenged in their learning;
- the desire to utilise creative approaches that enable every child to respond, contribute and lead;
- the need to create 'rich dialogues' that inspire children and staff;
- the desire to ensure that the children are seen as connected with the world and these connections are exploited and developed through reference to both the local and the global environment in which they live;
- the desire to ensure that the children are seen as a valuable resource for learning and for each other, and their own cultures, knowledge, experience and capabilities are respected and extended.

Who's who?

- *Asima Qureshi:* Deputy head, Dunkirk Primary School
- *Parmjit Sagoo:* Creative advisor and (drama) artist in residence, Dunkirk Primary School
- *Claire Simpson:* (Visual) artist in residence, Dunkirk Primary School
- *Jon Jenkins:* Year 1 class teacher, Dunkirk Primary School
- *Mark Woodings:* Year 2 class teacher, Dunkirk Primary School

Claire Simpson largely wrote this chapter, with contributions from Asima Qureshi and Parmjit Sagoo. Authors are indicated at the beginning of each section.

The school context and key issues

Asima Qureshi

- *Name:* Dunkirk Primary School
- *Location:* Nottingham, East Midlands
- *Age range:* 3–11
- *No. on roll:* approx 230

The children of Dunkirk represent an amazing range of countries, cultures, languages and religions. This is due to its proximity to Nottingham University and the hospital, both of whom attract many international students and employees. There are also many children from the local areas of Dunkirk, Radford and Lenton. This exciting combination of local and international families means that there is an extensive wealth of world knowledge within the school community. The school greatly values this diversity and is always seeking meaningful opportunities for children to develop dialogues which draw upon their different experiences within the world.

> Look at this description of the school written by Asima. Think about how you talk about your school and your children. What image of the child do you have in your school?
> Try to construct a new description of your school that highlights respect for children's cultures, knowledge, experience and capabilities.

Working in partnership with creative practitioners and external experts has evolved as a key way of achieving a high level of pupil motivation and engagement. Being part of Creative Partnerships since 2002 has formalised the management of this strategy in the school.

School ethos and 'big questions'

Claire Simpson

Asking 'big questions' has been central to developing dialogues between adults and young people. Prior to this project, the whole school had embarked upon an exploration which asked, 'What kind of a world do you want to live in?' The children talked passionately about many things they would like to see in the world including peace, more trees and less pollution. Their responses revealed a passionate interest in the issues that affect our world today and a desire to find out more about local and global issues.

It is within this context that the school developed the enquiry focus/question below:

> How can we develop a creative curriculum that nurtures the skills and qualities we need to be active, responsible citizens who are agents of change within our local and global community?

This question represents the school's key commitments to developing global citizenship, social responsibility, creativity and collaborative learning. Through the Creative Partnerships programme we hoped to continue creating rich dialogues, asking 'big questions' to inspire children and teachers to be curious about the world, to discuss, debate, imagine possibilities and investigate the issues that matter to them. In this project we wanted to develop this work and explore with them how they might effect change in the world – the philosophy of taking action, being active citizens and seeing how small steps add together to create something bigger.

> Here 'school ethos' is described as a variety of elements of the school. In light of this description consider:
> - how your own school ethos might or might not support the exploration of 'big questions';
> - what big questions you might want to ask your students.

What did we do?

Claire Simpson

Session 1: a provocation

The proposal to the children to begin the project was a huge pile of rubbish on the floor of the school hall – a provocation to prompt ideas. This involved both classes working together with the teachers and me for a whole morning session.

There were many responses we, as adults, hadn't predicted – the initial response of the Year 1 children particularly was: 'are we going to play with it?' 'are we going

Figure 5.1 The provocation, children and rubbish

to jump on it?' and especially: 'are we going to make things?' but then much discussion took place and several other children contributed ideas.

We asked the children 'how long has it taken us to collect this?' 'what's in this pile?' and eventually this led to a discussion around 'where will it go?' Some children suggested that the rubbish would go into a 'big hole' or that 'a truck comes along and takes it all away' – 'but where does the truck take it?' asked others. 'What happens then?' Some children felt that if the rubbish was put into the ground then it would turn back to soil, which led to a discussion around what else lives in the earth and could things in the pile of rubbish become compost. The Year 2 class regularly make compost and so were able to inject their knowledge about this.

The children then sorted the rubbish into groups of different materials. As they did so it was really interesting to see how the children responded to the things they were gathering. Many of the younger children naturally began to build with their materials or to line them up, or even to begin to wear them as costumes, making impromptu hats and bangles from containers. We looked at the different components of the pile of rubbish and talked about what could possibly be recycled. This conversation led to another discussion around what would be needed if we were going to turn all the plastic into other things: we'd need factories to do this – do we want more factories?

Another important impact of this initial session was that the children were trusted to be shown powerful images of animals killed by becoming caught up in plastic waste. This was placed in a context of asking the children to explore ways this could be changed. We talked about how these animal deaths could be prevented: 'It's better to die peacefully, than to die slowly in pain' said a Year 2 girl.

The children were bursting to talk after this initial session – their conversations were incredibly powerful and full of energy to take all this forward and we gathered ideas from them.

There is a culture in many UK schools of 'protecting' children from 'difficult' ideas. Would you feel happy showing children images of this nature? What would worry you and are there any solutions to your worries suggested in this chapter?

Finding infectious ideas: supporting core curriculum work

Sessions then took place with the classes separately, with each class following different (but linked) directions decided by the children and adults together.

Year 1 work

Year 1 were initially very excited by the possibilities of making things with the 'junk' so they undertook research into properties of different materials, exploring clay (real, rather than air-hardening), plasticine and 'junk'. They responded wonderfully to very hands-on, active, research and chatted away, noticing lots of things about the versatilities (or not) of different things: 'you need tape to fix the junk together, but when you put two pieces of clay together it just sticks'.

Year 2 work

The Year 2 class had been initially really struck by issues around plastic bags and had wanted to explore ways we could create bags from other materials. They designed and made bags from newspaper and also worked with a volunteer at the school to sew lost property clothes into bags. They undertook research into the properties and potential uses of different materials, testing for waterproof and weight-bearing potential.

One of the (many) unplanned elements of the project was the absorption by Year 2 in the story of the Midway Plastic Man. Claire had come across a set of BBC broadcasts from a reporter on Midway, a tiny island in the Pacific. These (available on-line) were taken to Year 2 to inject further ideas into the project and the children were completely captivated by one particular story. Midway is an important home for albatross colonies and is under threat from the vast amounts of rubbish found in the waters around the island and washed up onto the beaches. Scientists and conservationists are undertaking research there, and in clearing up the beaches had found a plastic toy warrior amongst the enormous piles of rubbish washed up.

The class were captivated by the idea of this toy. No children live on Midway or anywhere near there – where did the toy come from? How did he get there? What had happened to him on his journey to Midway?

Figure 5.2   Work in progress

Because it was a toy they made emotional connections with this piece of plastic. They wondered about the child or children who might have lost it: had someone dropped it from a boat when playing with it? Had a child lost it on a beach in another country? They began to think of the toy as a serial killer, theorising that it could be mistaken for food and eaten by an albatross (or turtle, or whale …), which would then suffocate and die; and once the bird's body had decomposed the plastic toy would be free to float away and kill another animal.

The children created very powerful pieces of writing as the issues around the plastic warrior proved to be superb for exploring characterisation. The children could identity with the lost toy in many different ways, some being pulled in by the ideas of toys coming to life and having adventures, others were drawn by the ideas of a child or children having lost their toy and why, others were hooked by issues around the welfare of sea-creatures. Their literacy work took the plastic warrior story in many different directions and covered several curriculum areas at the same time.

The children created storyboards to pull their ideas together into the story of the plastic warrior, some of which were used as part of their Year 2 SATS assessment. They then took their storyboards and created a stop-frame animation about the lost toy. They brought other toys in from home, holding auditions to find suitable figures to fulfil the roles in their film. They also created a wonderful array of clay and plasticine figures and told stories with these as they made them. The film was entered into a local authority competition where it won a runners-up award and has since been shown to many other adults and children. The children also all took copies home to share.

The project work also made direct links with science units for 5- and 6-year-olds as the children explored properties of different materials and issues around recycling.

Teachers and the artist skilfully drew on children's passions and interests which they linked in carefully with core curriculum work. What factors/elements of the way this project evolved have enabled them to do this successfully?

Making connections with local and global worlds

Opportunities to connect with the local area (as well as exploring wider global issues) were felt to be very important during the project. Both classes explored the immediate area around the school which included walking along the canal, a park, and some residential and industrial areas. This first-hand experience prompted lots of very interesting discussions. For example an interest in canal boats and the backs of houses seen from the towpath – as well as many discussions about the very evident rubbish. The natural world was evident everywhere too and the children eagerly found signs of this everywhere they looked.

Year 2 also visited a nearby supermarket to look at different packaging materials used to wrap up items for sale which generated lots of interesting discussions. Adults (staff and customers) in the supermarket asked us questions and were really interested in what we were doing there which gave the children an opportunity to articulate and speak with staff and with shoppers.

Figure 5.3 Children exploring next to the canal

Possibilities for the children to generate stories were everywhere, facilitated by the adults who were keen to make time for these opportunities to flourish. For example when walking by the canal several Year 2 children noticed a plastic rod sticking up out of the water. It would have been really easy to overlook this, but they were captivated by it and came up with the theory that this was a breathing tube for a fisherman who was underneath the water, snorkelling.

Sessions in the classroom enabled the children to explore their discoveries further. Many drawings emerged of the people who had thrown away some of the items we'd found – and models of trains, bridges and canals emerged. Children made puppets to enable them to create yet more stories around this. They also used toy creatures with junk materials to tell stories and explore ideas. 'I'm carrying out an experiment' one Year 1 boy announced as he tested out his hypotheses, placing toy insects inside a plastic bottle one at a time to see whether they would be able to get out safely if they fell in – or would they become stuck inside and die?

The willingness of staff and children to embark on off-site visits is bound up in the ethos of the school. From the Foundation Unit upwards children are regularly taken on walks and trips (more than weekly with some classes). Children are therefore used to walking as a group and thereby have a sense of awareness and safety when out together.

The diversity of the children at Dunkirk meant knowledge was brought in from across the globe. Many children have lived in different countries and were able to inject first-hand knowledge and anecdotes from other places. For instance, children brought in plastic toys from other countries, illustrating that the toy found on Midway could have come from anywhere in the world. Therefore for many of the children 'local' is also global and encompasses the whole world. Time for discussions as a class and in smaller groups was therefore incredibly important during the project.

> What is stopping you from taking children out of school? What kinds of changes might you make to make it easier for staff to do this more regularly?
>
> Using this chapter as a starting point consider the benefits for children's participation in taking children out of school and making links with your local community in this way.

Valuing the children's concerns and finding ways to take action

After some time working on the project the children decided they wanted to create a protest march about plastic bag use and rubbish. We then spent some time working on designs and discussing ways of conveying information and creating impact. The atmosphere in the classroom was a constant buzz as we all exchanged ideas, debated and engaged with the themes being explored. The children spent a lot of time sharing their work with each other, showing a genuine interest in each other's ideas.

Figure 5.4 Children working together

Ideas flew around. Designs for protest t-shirts were drawn onto t-shirt-shaped paper which then became something to play with as the children experimented with ways of cutting a piece of paper into a t-shirt shape and wanted to wear their paper designs. They also discovered that the off-cuts were in the shape of tiny t-shirts and explored designing t-shirts for toys and pets from these.

Their designs and slogans for t-shirts and bags were both hand-drawn and also designed in the ICT suite and transferred onto fabric with special paper. Every design was different and every design had an impact: 'Do you want a clean world? – save the world from being boring', 'We are heroes, we don't drop plastic bags.'

The children were serious about their concerns and wanted to have their voice heard. The project culminated in a joint sharing of work with other schools which took the form of a protest march designed by the children. We marched through a very visible route in Nottingham to a prominent venue (Wollaton Hall), finishing back at school to demonstrate in front of everyone in the school. 'I can't believe it's finally coming to life' said one 6-year-old girl as we set off from school.

Taking part in an actual protest held a sense of real empowerment and strength for both the children and the adults. Unprompted, the children burst into spontaneous chants as they walked through the streets carrying their banners. Traffic had to stop to let the procession pass through pedestrian crossings and many vehicles sounded their horns in support – which added to the children's sense of reaching a wider public. When we arrived back at school there was a whole school assembly and the two classes marched into the school hall loudly chanting and proudly waving banners, bags, placards and windmills. There was a sense of celebrating the children's work and concerns at a whole school level.

Figure 5.5 Children working on their designs

Figure 5.6 Child protestors

What role do adults have in ensuring children's voices are heard? Consider what needs to be thought through in ensuring that children's creative participation work has an audience. For example, child protection, form and/or technology. Who is the right audience?

Partnerships between adults and between adults and children

The project artist, Claire Simpson, is committed to working in partnerships on projects which enable children and adults together to investigate, research, ask questions and explore hypotheses; with this sitting alongside reflective pedagogical documentation that seeks to find ways to record children's learning.

Clare Simpson writes …

I had worked with children and staff at Dunkirk on previous projects exploring aspects of global citizenship which this project drew on. I had developed a good working relationship with the school, having found a shared ethos and approach with staff and I continue to work there as a resident artist with the foundation unit and through projects across other year groups.

I felt (and continue to feel) a strong bond with the school. As a freelancer it can sometimes be hard to step into different educational settings; and the approach of an artist seeking to investigate can sometimes be at odds with the approach of some schools if they tend towards more rigid structures and pre-determined outcomes. Dunkirk has a very open and welcoming ethos and is an exceptionally friendly school; this nurturing atmosphere gives support and that becomes a two-way exchange.

Between the adults there was a shared joy in the journey of working with children and listening to their discoveries. There was also a shared willingness to explore both materials and complex issues, and wanting children to have a very active hands-on approach in their investigations.

The project had a loose outline drawn up by the adults that set out ideas about what might happen. We wanted the children to shape the project with us but also wanted to ensure we had a set of ideas and resources ready to draw upon where needed. We weren't working to set lesson plans or formats but, informally, we had aims and objectives for each session. We needed to be realistic in terms of what was going to give a sense of discovery and success for everyone, but also what would be achievable with a whole class. For example, when making bags, we didn't give out templates or dictate ways materials had to be used, but we suggested techniques (appropriate to the dexterity of the children) and had collected many examples and certain tools and resources that would help. We trusted ourselves and the children and set the classroom up in specific ways (for example, children chose and then fetched their own equipment as and when they needed it).

As adults we all talked about how much we had learnt during the project. We felt it was important to let the children know that we don't have all the answers but that we are constantly researching and asking questions ourselves too.

Deep partnerships were built and these continue now. As the project enabled a lot of discussions and reflections to take place, adults and children were able to get to know each other well and to build a strong bond and sense of community.

Dunkirk value the partnerships they have developed and see them as contributing to the creation of a more meaningful learning environment for their pupils. What seem to be the benefits of working with other adults in a long term capacity? How often do you get to work collaboratively with other adults in this way?

Documentation

Claire's documenting, charting, recording and gathering evidence throughout the project has enabled us to see the long journeys that were made by many of the children. Some exceptionally profound moments and pieces of work were created and the children used words and images to explore their feelings in a very sophisticated and moving way.

For example, when creating designs for protest t-shirts, one boy showed me his design, full of wonderful drawings and a slogan he'd written which he softly read out to me: 'It says "save the world from being a cold-hearted place".' It was an important moment because it hadn't been immediately easy to read this boy's handwriting and he often worked quietly by himself. The project provided a format and classroom set-up which enabled the adults to take time to talk to

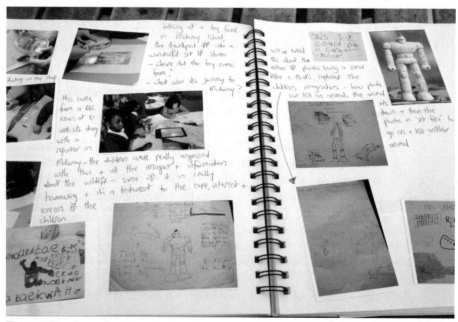

Figure 5.7 Journal pages

and hear this boy's words – partly because there were more adults in the room but also because the children were taking ownership of their own learning in new ways.

The thoughts and ideas of both adults and children were recorded session-by-session through the project journal which in turn was a tool for reflection. I used both photography and the children's own words, pictures and writing to create this journal that was then used as a tool for reflection with children and staff and placed in the classroom as a permanent record of the project for children and staff members.

What are the benefits of taking this kind of approach to documentation and reflection? How might this kind of approach require you to re-prioritise your own time (e.g. it would be important to ensure you had enough time to record and listen for student responses but also that time was set aside to review the material collected and its meaning in any assertions of impact)?

Dunkirk's model of 'co-production of learning'

Claire Simpson

Editor's note: Dunkirk's model of co-production draws on the philosophies of learning adopted in Reggio Emilia schools in Italy. Fundamental to the Reggio approach is the image of the child as rich in potential, strong, curious and competent. Children are encouraged to develop their own theories about the world and how it works and to explore these collaboratively. Each child is valued for their different experiences, ideas and opinions, and listening involves being open to what others have to say.[1]

Dunkirk's model of co-production is based on a belief that the children would shape the direction of the project with the adults. Co-production in this project included:

- Valuing the role and existing skills and experiences of both the children and the adults.
- The project wasn't about a linear progression from point A to point B which had been pre-determined by adults. The adults were keen to find infectious ideas with the children which could develop and be explored in different directions.
- Investigating together and seeing projects as being an opportunity for adults and children to share ideas and to research together.
- The adults involved have a gentle, respectful and open approach and genuinely seek to listen to children – combined with a sense of enjoyment and shared humour. This involved time to listen with all the senses (especially so given that this project took place with 5- and 6-year-old pupils). It's not about

simply asking children what they want to do – it requires adults who are skilled at listening to children, who are able to reflect and unravel and who are able to inject open-ended questions and resources in response to the children's enquiries.

- A willingness from adults to embrace the complexities of developing directions in learning together. As adults we wanted to encourage questioning rather than providing straightforward answers for the children; we wanted to set up environments for exploring, testing out ideas, posing theories and for discovery.

- Time for children to conduct hands-on research and learn and develop theories through doing, without adults jumping in to answer the children's questions before they've even had a chance to form them.

- Time for reflection (with the children and also between the adults) after each session and that each new session began with adults and children together re-capping on what had happened so far and exploring future directions of the project.

- Pedagogical documentation: keeping an on-going record of the project – trying to gather pedagogical documentation that would record the children's thoughts, actions and ideas so that we could reflect, listen and respond. We also wanted to record our own thoughts throughout the project. A journal was kept with notes and images being added during every session – not as a neat document but as a working tool.

Can you identify the key elements of the Dunkirk model of co-production from this description? Does this match your own idea of what 'co-production' means? Is there anything missing from this description? What might be the practical implications of developing this kind of approach to learning? Does anything surprise you?

Editor's note – what is co-production (also known as 'co-construction')?

Co-production is variously understood in the literature. As a starting point co-production is an 'asset based' approach that involves a recognition that each learner brings his or her own expertise into the classroom which should be valued. Teachers and students work closely together to share their expertise and build learning together. The idea is that this in turn builds reciprocity and mutual respect between students and teachers – as both become learners and, at times, teachers. Some educators understand 'co-production' as involving young people more in lessons that the teachers themselves plan, however the Dunkirk model goes beyond this in that their students develop a sense of ownership and control over what is learnt, how it is learnt and when it is learnt, at least in this creative learning project. Concepts such as 'exploratory pedagogy' and 'negotiated pedagogy' may offer more concrete strategies for schools who are interested in pursuing this type of approach to learning, and extending their students' role in curriculum decision making.[2]

What happened next?

Parmjit Sagoo

For the children that were involved in 'Small Action – Big Change' the experience did not end there. The project has stayed with the children in different ways. Many continue to use the bags and t-shirts they made and still have a strong connection with the issues explored in the project. Two years later pupils continue to draw upon things learnt during the project; an example being a recent clean-up event along the canal attended by members of the Eco-club,[3] who readily recalled many of the issues that arose when they visited the canal as part of the project.

Children continue to consider big questions connected to global issues as they move through the school. This has included the setting up and running of a fictional pet rescue centre as a response to animal cruelty, an issue that the children identified themselves as a key issue that needs changing. A drama artist and the Year 3 teacher who worked with the children on this enterprise said that they could clearly see the impact their previous creative experiences had on their ability to discuss, debate and find imaginative solutions to problems posed to them within the pet rescue centre.

The project and the learning that took place through the process has been disseminated in a number of ways. For instance, it was shared within the school through assemblies, displays, staff meetings and parents' events. These sharing events have created many interesting discussions about pupil voice and the role of 'questioning' (particularly 'big questions') within the learning process.

The project has also reached a wider audience through being used as an example of good practice when visitors from other schools and organisations come to the school. It was also a key part of a regional global citizenship conference in July 2009. This conference involved a group of Dunkirk pupils facilitating the opening session of the conference during which they posed their own questions to the teacher delegates about global citizenship and social responsibility. This group of around ten pupils call themselves the 'Advocates' and continue to represent the school at key events within and outside the school. There are also many other groups in school that support and expand pupil voice and the children's global awareness, including the school Eco club and the debating group. Due to the children's and teacher's passion about the environment, two Foundation Stage teachers are doing Forest School training, an educational approach/philosophy which places pupil voice, nature and the environment at its heart.

The school continues to invest in collaborative and creative learning through employing two artists for a regular day a week. These artists are an integral part of the school community and work in partnership with teachers and children. They are involved in many aspects of school life including curriculum development.

Creative Partnerships projects such as Small Action – Big Change need the full support and understanding of the management in school. If a teacher is to allow the pupils to mould and dictate where their learning is going, he/she must feel free to decide what elements of the curriculum for that term can be changed, dropped or postponed. One strategy which is now used every term is for the curriculum coordinator to work alongside all staff to review the forthcoming term's planning. Discussions are held between teachers, teaching assistants and creative practitioners about what issues are current and where pupils show a particular interest.

The posing of 'big questions' is now more present within the school's curriculum planning and we are currently exploring how we can develop a curriculum which is driven and inspired by 'big questions'. These questions have the potential to be generated by any member of the school community, including children, teachers, artists and parents. Some of this work has involved our link school in Pakistan which has also explored some of the same 'big questions'. These responses have been shared across the two schools, creating a fascinating and deep dialogue about the world we live in, a dialogue which taps into the children's beliefs, values and visions for the future.

Professional development questions

First, this chapter describes a collaborative, mutual approach to children's participation which is embedded in learning processes within the school. Compare this approach with the models we have seen described in the work in secondary schools (Chapters 2 and 4). Could this kind of approach work in secondary schools too? List any advantages of this approach, barriers to integrating this kind of approach in secondary schools and possible solutions.

Advantages	Potential barriers	Possible solutions
For example... Draws on children's lives outside school	Time/curriculum constraints	Re-designing curriculum to allow time for young people to draw on their own cultures, lives and experiences

Second, Claire has suggested a range of questions that you might usefully ask to staff:

- What image of the child do you have in your school?
- What are the issues around modern childhood?
- What does it mean to be a child in our world – what are the challenges and tasks within this?
- What big questions do you ask the children and yourselves?
- What support networks exist for you as an adult working with children?
- Where do you draw your influences and inspirations from?
- How often do you take time to reflect, revisit and discuss these issues?

Staff could work in groups to discuss the questions and represent their discussion in words or pictures on a large sheet of paper.

Notes

1 For more on Reggio Emilia see L. Thornton and P. Brunton. (2009) (2nd edn) *Understanding the Reggio Approach*. London: David Fulton Press; and C. Rinaldi (2005) *In Dialogue with Reggio Emilia: Listening, Researching and Learning*. London: Routledge.

2 See P. Thomson, K. Jones and C. Hall (2009) *Final Report: Creative School Change Research Project*. London: Creative Partnerships. Available at http://www.creativitycultureeducation.org/research-impact/thematic-research/

3 The Eco club was a group of children who met regularly with a teacher to discuss and act on environment issues.

References

Rinaldi, C. (2005) *In Dialogue with Reggio Emilia: Listening, Researching and Learning*. London: Routledge.

Thomson, P., Jones, K. and Hall, C. (2009) *Final Report: Creative School Change Research Project*. London: Creative Partnerships. Available at http://www.creativitycultureeducation.org/research-impact/thematic-research/

Thornton, L. and Brunton, P. (2009) (2nd edn) *Understanding the Reggio Approach*. London: David Fulton Press.

6

Creative islands
Creative approaches to inclusion and voice

Ben Edwards, Three Ways School

Chapter overview

This chapter focuses on how creative practices may enable a wider range of views to be sought and expressed, particularly in non-verbal or less formal ways. The example from Three Ways School, Bath, in the south-west of the UK focuses on how the teachers worked with creative practitioners to create a physical and social space for creative and participative work. The range of sensory inputs experienced in the physical space of the project, combined with enough time to make their own decisions and listen to others, helped the learners and teachers to overcome their initial self-consciousness, to take on different identities and engage in and experiment with different forms of learning. The elements of their challenge can be characterised as:

- the difficulties in immersing all children in the curriculum, especially in a climate of increased personalisation of learning;
- the need to develop and apply an innovative model of curriculum delivery that would engage all of our learners;
- challenging teacher identities and roles in changing relations between learners and teachers;
- engaging young people with perceived 'low levels' of motivation for learning and participation;
- helping learners to feel part of the process of learning, rather than one of its products.

Who's who?

- *The students:* Six male students identified as being disengaged with elements of the curriculum and at times disaffected by the learning process
- *Ben Edwards:* A secondary class teacher, Three Ways School, who delivered the weekly sessions
- *Adrian Snell:* Music therapist (a composer and creative arts consultant), Three Ways School
- *Judy Dumont:* Sensory support teacher, Three Ways School
- *Sue Mower:* ICT technician, Three Ways School

Ben Edwards wrote this chapter about his experiences as a teacher leading this project.

The school context and key issues

- *Name:* Three Ways School
- *Location:* Bath, UK
- *Age range:* 5–18
- *No. on roll:* 158

Three Ways School is a purpose built SEN school that supports children and young adults with a range of special educational needs. Our pupils' challenges are as varied as they are complex. We work alongside children with profound and multiple learning difficulties (PMLD), severe learning difficulties (SLD), children with autistic spectrum disorder (ASD), moderate learning difficulties (MLD) and children with a range of challenging behaviours. The school works with a dedicated team of teachers, teaching assistants, a music therapist, speech and language therapists, physiotherapists, multi-agency professionals and a range of creative practitioners.

The school is the product of three amalgamated Special Educational Needs (SEN) schools each with different student populations with their own unique set of strengths and challenges. Considering the diverse nature of our school population, it would have been folly to adopt a one dimensional, overly prescriptive approach to teaching and learning.

At Three Ways School in Bath, it is our mission to provide an environment where children not only feel safe but excited to creatively explore their full learning potential. Paramount to this is the flexibility and freedom that staff have to personalise the curriculum to serve the needs of the individual.

Whilst having this extremely varied set of learning needs in one setting may be particular to SEN schools, it is true to say that the methods employed to support all our learners are equally relevant to mainstream settings where increasingly diverse learning populations abound.

We follow the UK National Curriculum and adapt our teaching to facilitate access to achievement for every student. Staff work closely with our pupils employing multi-sensory approaches to learning which seek to engage the body as much as they do the mind. The term 'multi-sensory' has been used to refer to activities that 'combine two or more sensory strategies to take in or express information' (QIA 2008, p.2).[1] As a term it has been connected with the debate around 'learning styles' and the suggestion here is that in appealing to a person's preferred learning style or addressing more than one learning style, knowledge acquisition and retention will be more effective.

Through this holistic way of working, we believe our students are able to connect with and process their learning on a much deeper and more meaningful level. Pupils are actively encouraged to gain ownership of their learning with the specific intention of creating school leavers who go on to being independent lifelong learners. To this end, pupil voice can be heard throughout our school from its physical structure, filtering through collaborative curriculum design, pupils' self-directed target setting, the development of pupil-centred life skills programmes to governance through the school council.

> There are many ideas circulating in schools about learning styles – questions such as 'How many learning styles are there?' or 'How can we account for students' different learning styles?' abound. Watch this video http://www.youtube.com/watch?v=iYgO8jZTFuQ and consider whether Gardner's notion of 'Multiple Intelligences' (Gardner, 1993) is a useful addition to the debate. Nick Owen's book in this series also addresses some of these issues (Owen, 2011).

Fig 6.1 Three Ways School

The Creative Islands project engaged a group of male students in a multi-sensory learning experience in which they worked with their teacher and two creative practitioners, enacting a shipwreck, over a period of five weeks. The students at the centre of this project presented with low self-esteem and demonstrated a lack of confidence in approaching unfamiliar challenges. The boys each experienced literacy and numeracy difficulties and had interpersonal skills which restricted their access to collaborative working experiences. Furthermore, they frequently presented with low levels of motivation when invited to take ownership of their learning. These were students whose experiences of a mainstream curriculum have been characterised by a catalogue of failures and a sense of learned helplessness rendering them fearful of taking risks and experimenting with their learning. Of greatest significance here is that these were the very pupils whose communication styles offered them a voice but a voice seldom attended to by their peers and at times one which served to alienate them from the wider community.

Consider the students involved in this project and how they came to be involved. How might this be viewed by the young people themselves as well as by other young people in the school?

Working with creative practitioners

Throughout the process, the teacher worked collaboratively with creative practitioners. In the planning phase, these practitioners were a spark that ignited the ideas of staff and students involved in the scheme. In addition to this, creative practitioners were at liberty to challenge the preconceived ideas and expectations of staff with fresh perspectives on pupil capabilities. Furthermore, in developing fresh perspectives, staff were encouraged to try out more experimental approaches to the activities. The opportunity for reflective dialogue between staff and creative practitioners played a vital part in preparing sessions to address the needs of all students. In addition, this dialogue enabled staff to acknowledge the more incidental learning elements to the project and how these represented certain milestones in the progress of key groups and individuals.

Negotiating a 'space' for the project: pupil motivation and collaborative planning

Students were initially selected by key workers on the grounds of who might benefit most from this set of experiences. At first the students were given some idea of how the project would progress and their willingness to participate gauged. A consistent time and place were agreed for the sessions which would take place in the sprawling cellar complex of a Georgian manor house formerly known as Summerfield School. Following on from the 'Around the World in 30 Days' theme of a previous project, it was decided that we would base these sessions loosely around a journey. The students debated potential destinations and how they would get there. Eventually the group decided they would travel to South America by ship. Thanks to their leanings towards all things macabre, disaster would strike and the ship would sink leaving only six surviving crew and the captain stranded on a desert island. This is where our story begins.

A key factor in the success of this project was the time allocated to prepare a motivating and engaging set of learning experiences for the students. It was important to consult with students in the design phase of their learning journey to offer a sense of empowerment and ownership of their learning. Collaborative planning with students and creative practitioners offered a different perspective on the structure of the project and compelled staff to raise their expectations injecting the process with fresh energy.

In this chapter the learners were consulted about how they wanted the project to develop even before it began. How often do you work collaboratively with learners, or indeed other colleagues, at this stage in a project in making decisions about the shape and place of their learning? Can you think of ways that you might make time and 'space' within school for these kinds of discussions?

A consistent place, space and routine

We found that framing these creative learning approaches within a consistent structure and predictable routine allayed the fears and reduced the anxieties that many of these learners carry with them in relation to unfamiliar and intimidating tasks. It was noticed that increased levels of anticipation fed directly into the group's enthusiasm to take on tasks and sustain their focus. It became clear that students needed to feel secure in themselves and in their relationships with staff and peers in order to engage in the learning. A consistently available time and space to carry out the project was essential especially in the early days of the project as it gave the students a predictable variable upon which they could rely. It was noted that only when pupils were fully relaxed and had left their negative experiential and emotional baggage at the door were they were truly able to access and refine their full repertoire of skills and begin to explore new ones.

Consider other ways that you may enable students to move away from negative school based identities. (How) might creative approaches draw attention to affective dimensions and thereby support such identity work?

How did we do this?

The sessions began with the teacher greeting the students in their class with paraffin lamp in hand, a salty sea dog air about him and a fairly outrageous tricorn hat to top it all off. From this point, it was all six hands on deck and down into the cellar they would descend. Once below deck, an air of anticipation was created with low candle light and the sounds of a creaking ship echoing all around them. Pupils were encouraged to share their mood verbally or through the use of symbols, to ascertain the emotional state of each participant, and acknowledge the starting place for their journeys. Some students decided to elaborate on this and gave reasons for their mood but for others, the process of sharing their feelings was enough. The structure of the session was shared using visual symbols as well as the written word. Once the group was secure with the outline for the session, a short theme tune was sung to the group with their names written into the lyrics. It was amazing to observe how quickly these streetwise teenagers evolved from a sniggering, resistant cluster during the first session to whole-hearted participants in the experience as the weeks went on.

It is sometimes assumed that learners will enjoy a creative or different approach to learning. However, Ben here suggests that emotions such as 'fear' could disrupt such activities if not anticipated and tackled. Can you think of a time when this has happened in your school? How could you have alleviated these problems or enabled students to discuss their concerns?

What we did: a journey with our learners

In this section Ben goes into some detail about what each session involved. We should note that he worked in close collaboration with the creative practitioners involved in the delivery of this project – this involved intensive joint planning sessions as well as a substantial amount of preparation work before each session began.

Week 1: all aboard

During this introductory session, pupils were recruited to join a voyage to South America. Every pupil was given a Hessian sack for their belongings and was expected to fill out a short contract using a quill and ink pot. We discussed the feelings that people would have leaving port on long voyages and what items they would take with them if they could only take five items from home.

The sensory input in this session ranged from the smell of brine from tinned tuna through to the cedar oil from an aromatherapy burner to give the scent of a ship's timbers. Pupils tasted dried fish, flagons of shandy, limes to ward off scurvy and pickled vegetables as part of their life on board. Visual footage of ships departing port and the dockside in Bristol were used to set the scene accompanied by the sounds of working docks and seagulls amassing overhead. Pupils were given the task of plaiting rope and scrubbing the decks before the lights faded and projections of a starry night were displayed to signify time to retire. The session then closed with a final playing of the theme tune and an uncharacteristically calm return to class.

In later conversations with their class teacher it was revealed that a number of the students were exceptionally reluctant to commit pen to paper yet the novelty of this writing exercise was enough to encourage full participation. The students were clearly self-conscious for the first part of the session and took a little time to lose themselves in the experience. It was the first time I had seen these students paying full attention to one another, allowing each other adequate space and time to consider their choices. The pupils were thoroughly amused by the effects of limes and dried fish on those crewmates with slightly more delicate palates! Three years down the line, these pupils can still recall why the British Navy used to take limes on long voyages with them.

Week 2: stormy seas

In the second session pupils seemed a little more excited as their captain press ganged them from their regular class. All pupils were given their hessian sacks and this week every sack had a torch inside. Instead of the comforting sounds of waves lapping against a ship in port, pupils were met by the clap of thunder and the howl of gale force winds. It is worth noting here that teacher voice was kept to a minimum to support pupil contribution and the development of different styles of interaction and communication. A specific element of this session was the exploration of Morse code as a method of communication, with students practising their techniques on one another.

As the voyage progressed, images of brewing storm clouds were projected onto the wall of the cellar. Constructed sails billowed wildly in response to a carefully positioned wind machine and the crew rocked in unison to port, starboard, stern and bow. As the storm drew closer pupils were given African Djembe drums to replicate the sounds of rain and thunder. As the storm grew in intensity, videos of tempestuous seas were projected and pupils were sprayed lightly with salt water. The boat became unstable and SOS signals were made using the Morse code studied earlier in the session. At the cry of 'abandon ship', the students jumped from their vessel, accompanied, controversially by their captain who was quite happy to break with convention on this occasion.

The crew appeared more attentive to the visual timetable and were able to predict the running order prior to our discussion. For the first time, the group showed signs of having become fully immersed in the activity, and were playing collaboratively without even realising it.

How important is it that young people are offered a range of modes for communicating (such as using Morse code, playing collaboratively) in your setting? Do you think it would enhance your learners' sense of having a voice (in secondary as well as in primary schools) if you made more use of different modes, forms and technologies of communication in learning?

Table 6.1 An example lesson plan

Week 2	Date:	Theme: Stormy seas
Starters	Start away from room to set scene and establish notion of structure through pupil/staff dialogue. Feelings and checking in through mood tree. Brain gym to engage pupils. Share symbols to offer pupils insight into session structure. Hand out sacks with torches inside. Line up outside the cellar, wait for silence.	
Materials	*Items:* oil and rags in margarine boxes, sails, rigging, gang plank, boxes, sacks, blankets, barrel, torches, wind machine. *Memento:* torch. *Audio-visual:* storm sequences, perfect storm DVD, images of old sailors, water projection, thunder and lightning from projector and sounds from CD, image of island in darkness. *Symbols*: silence, bring up the gang plank, sitting, smells, watching, action, night and day, sleep, close.	
Theme Song (Hello)	Based on 'Kate Rusby I Courted a Sailor': Oh I'm bound for the waves, the waves dearest Annie, I'm bound for the waves, the waves upon the sea. Oh I'm bound for the waves, the waves dearest Annie, I'm bound for the waves, the captain calls me. (Supplement Annie with names of pupils.)	
Taste/smell/touch/ action	*Smell:* brine from tuna tins, spray salt water from garden dispensers. *Touch and action:* Hessian sacks, boxes to load, gang plank to pull in, anchor to pull in. Morse code for SOS to tune of SOS on guitar to sound of Morse code in background. Rocking to port, starboard, bow and stern. Draw in the sails, pulling ropes, secure items.	
Audio-visual	*Audio:* sounds of distant thunder, waves, billowing sails, creaking of ship. *Visual:* project images of water lapping on to roof, images of clouds building, storm brewing with thunder and lightning.	
Taste/smell/touch/ action	*Smell:* wood smells from shavings and sanding pine, wax smells from furniture wax. Oil from oily rags. *Touch and action:* hand drums to begin to make sounds of storm, building sounds to crescendo. Abandon ship, grab sack and find space in room to view projected images of sinking ship and storm from cast-away, douse the oil lamps. *Taste:* salt water.	
Audio-visual	*Audio:* sounds of water, creaking ship, breaking of wood, cries for help, SOS, Lord's prayer recited as part of recording. *Visual:* water and sea projection, distant island to swim to.	
Theme song (goodbye)	See above.	
Review	Homework: bring one piece of music you would want to have with you on a desert island.	
Leaving	Collect sacks from pupils and place their sacks back in the trunk.	

Week 3: marooned

The students were keen to re-engage with the activity from last week having ended the activity spying an island from where their ship had sunk. Pupils had been set a homework task of bringing one desert island disc to share with their peers. Never have I seen a group so keen to complete their homework! There was some surprise in the group to find the room filled with sand, palm trees swaying in the breeze and a scattering of shells and coconuts.

The pupils were asked to cut up and distribute various tropical fruits to their shipmates. Following this, the group was set a challenge of breaking open a coconut and extracting the milk. This precipitated a lively group discussion with all manner of potential solutions suggested. Finally, the group was able to reach a democratic decision and elected for some carefully placed blows to the coconut with a rock. When the challenge was finally completed, all members of the group were keen to celebrate their very real success with a toast of the coconut milk that remained.

This session was characterised by a much higher level of cooperation between the group members. Generally speaking, the group indicated a more positive emotional state through the established starter activity which may speak of a greater level of security felt towards the programme, their ship mates or indeed within themselves. By now, the pupils were familiar with the established routines and took a good deal of pleasure, smiling openly at hearing their names being sung at the start and close of every session.

It was a real privilege to witness the play which ensued with all students totally engaged in exploring the texture of the fine sand and developing their own shapes and patterns. This outcome was entirely serendipitous and could not have been foreseen by prior planning or facilitated by pre-determined outcome driven activities. This example of incidental learning is the very reason why explorative creative activities such as these sessions are so valuable for our students. Not only did this activity provide these students with a therapeutic space in which to explore their learning in safety, it gave them an opportunity to still their minds and access their own voices often hidden by insecurity and ingrained patterns of negative behaviour.

Week 4: island life

Having taken of the fruits of island life, it was time to get on with the practicalities of being marooned on a desert island. The sand proved to be popular again and students were faced with the task of creating their own shell necklaces using materials found in boxes washed ashore on the beach. The group explored their own sense of identity and demonstrated developing self-reflective skills. This was proceeded by a discussion of how being marooned for a prolonged period of time could begin to affect your sense of self. The students spoke about group identity and how supporting the same football team as your friends could bring you closer. They linked the idea of a strong group identity being of importance in difficult circumstances and suggested that a good start might be to develop a set of similar identity necklaces.

Having been united by their experiences within the confines of the cellar space, it was decided to see if the group could begin to generalise their motivated and cooperative working styles to other areas of the school. As the virtual rain began to fall indoors, the students were given the task of building a shelter outside in the school grounds. All of the tools and many useful materials were unearthed from the boxes washed ashore in the sand. Roles were shared between the group based on a combination of self-evaluation and peer-to-peer evaluation of each candidate and available roles. Before heading out to the rainforest to develop their shelter, all remaining crew helped to compose and write a short message to be placed in a bottle and cast out to sea in the hope of rescue. By this point, the pupils were literally organising the visual schedule for themselves; such were their levels of motivation. There was a definite change in the levels of motivation to engage with the work demonstrated by the group, evident in their increasing desire to participate and contribute to the activities.

> Why was it important that this group developed a strong group identity? How did this affect their 'voices' when the project was taken out of their 'safe' project space and into the school?

Week 5: SOS and rescue

Pupils began the session as normal and were highly motivated by the shelter-building exercise from the previous week. Some of the students had been developing the shelter in their free time between sessions and had constructed an elaborate design based on a survivalist's template. The group shared their plans with one another and the teacher.

Having returned to camp the group were drawn to lighting a fire in preparation for cooking potatoes found in the undergrowth. Conversation soon moved to the project and how they would have liked to continue with this work every week.

Attention shifted from the fire to a ship on the horizon skippered by the deputy head, signal flag in hand. The group began to generate their own smoke signals based on the Morse code learned earlier in the programme to great effect. As the vessel drew nearer one student turned and asked if they really had to go as they preferred life on the island. The teacher replied that now they knew where the island was, they could always come back to it.

It was quite remarkable to see how settled members of the group became as the fire grew in intensity and they began to place their potatoes. Group members were able to evaluate their own contributions which, in turn, were confirmed by their peers who were much more ready to offer praise for activities perceived to be invested with meaning and significance.

Key learning

Increasing student voice through participation in explorative, creative learning activities

Increased levels of student voice and motivation may be attributed to the explorative learning activities typified by this project. Here experiential learning, where pupils work with and manipulate objects and situations, offers a more effective teaching and learning method than concentration on content, where the pupils are expected to memorise information. Furthermore, in seeking new pathways of learning for our students, multi-sensory teaching approaches have encouraged students to engage more deeply with their learning and develop a participatory voice. Being able to focus on experimentation, innovation and original thought within the context of these sessions drew staff and pupils' foci away from measurable outcomes towards individual creativity, imagination and the courage to feel part of the learning process rather than just another of its products. As teachers adopt these methods they may change their perceptions of young people, appealing to more than just their minds. Young people are then more likely to develop a voice more clearly linked to their holistic, lived experiences of the world.

> Ben suggests that this investigation revealed that this kind of learning is not the sole reserve of students with PMLD or SLD but that there are much wider applications for students in both SEN and mainstream schools. Do you agree? If so, what might these applications be in your school?

Teacher and student roles

The teachers and creative practitioners here created a space in which adults and students were able to work outside normal classroom rules and expectations. For example, through dressing up, the teacher took a step back from his usual role as a teacher. The room was decorated to motivate the students and other (multisensory) stimulations helped to transport them to another place. This enabled the participants – both students and teachers – to experiment with new classroom roles.

> Pressures of curriculum and assessment can make it difficult for teachers to develop relationships with young people in which they find out about 'young people's worlds' and in which young people find out more about each other. What is it about this project that has enabled this to happen? Would it be possible to do something similar in your own setting?

Different modes, forms and technologies for voice

Through this project, it became clear that students are equally open to, and at times prefer non-verbal communication strategies, for instance they enjoyed using Morse code, African drumming and making shell necklaces to express their thoughts and identities. Thus, words became one communication avenue but did not form the sole route to the learning destination. It was agreed by all participants that this way of working facilitated the expression and development of pupil voice more readily than any other approach.

Relations between young people and between teachers and young people

A key variable was the strength of relationships within the project. Pupils were much more willing to engage with self-assessment and peer-to-peer evaluation once they had become secure in their relationships with other participants.

So often it is the teacher's voice that dominates planning discussions and it was as much of a lesson for the teacher in discovering the true capabilities of the group as it was for the group in discovering their own talents. As instructors, some teachers have learned to allow their voices to dominate classroom environments. In getting to work more closely with the students, teachers were offered a much clearer route of entry into young peoples' worlds and ultimately a better understanding of individual students.

What next?

Following on from earlier research into the effects of multi-sensory experiential learning opportunities on pupil progress and development, whole school curriculum change ensued as the three separate sites united under one roof. Multi-sensory approaches are interwoven throughout the curriculum and figure highly as part of our on-going commitment to staff and whole school development. The school has constructed a state of the art sensory studio on site where technology and creative teaching meet, generating spectacular learning opportunities.

We are in the process of further collaborative projects with creative practitioners ranging from robotics experts to fashion designers who support our on-going defiance of the boundaries imposed on our learners by their own expectations and the expectations harboured by wider society. We will continue to challenge the assumption that all children arrive with a single general intelligence or learning style and that one model of curriculum delivery will fit all. We are strongly supportive of the view that everyone possesses a unique combination of different abilities which can and will change in relation to their experiences and opportunities.

Professional development questions

Access and inclusion: this project engaged a targeted small group of young people who clearly benefited from and enjoyed the project. Consider (and list) the pros and cons of this kind of approach and think through alternative ways of getting young people involved.

Teacher and student identities were disrupted in this project. What kinds of strategies were important in this project in encouraging learners (and teachers) to move away from their previous school identities and roles?

Ben suggested that the staff involved learnt how important it is to record aspects of learning you might not usually consider. What kind of research/documentation practices could help you to identify this key but often 'incidental' learning in your school?

This chapter suggests that schools may increase inclusion in student voice activities through offering young people opportunities to communicate in different ways. What forms, technologies might work to enable greater inclusion in student voice activities in your school?

Note

1   Quality and Improvement Agency (QIA) (2008) Multisensory learning. Available at tlp. excellencegateway.org.uk/tlp/.../qs_multi_sensory_learning.pdf

References

Gardner, H. (1993) (10th edition) *Frames of Mind: The Theory of Multiple Intelligences.* New York: Basic Books.

Owen, N. (2011) *Developing A Creative Curriculum: Innovative Teachers at Work.* London: David Fulton Press.

Room 13
Children in charge of a creative space on the margins

Neil Small, West Rise Junior School

Chapter overview

This chapter explores a 'Room 13' initiative in a primary school setting in Eastbourne situated in the South East of the UK. The first 'Room 13' was set up in 1994, at Caol Primary School in Scotland (www.room13scotland.com). It was developed by children working with artist Rob Fairley and has since grown into an international network. Whilst practice varies according to setting and context, Room 13s generally have two distinctive features. First, a professional artist in residence shares a studio space with young people, doing her or his own work but also engaging with the students who attend; second, the studio is run by young people, with a student committee taking responsibility for its daily organisation (ordering supplies, ensuring it is well maintained and harmonious) and fundraising to meet, at a minimum, the studio's running costs. As a concept, then, Room 13 draws on notions of creativity as both a discipline and a 'right', of creative professionalism and social/business enterprise, in which children play a central and equal role. (Rob Fairley comments that he prefers to talk about 'adults of different ages' rather than adults and children.)[1]

The elements of the school's challenge in this chapter can be identified as:

- Supporting young people to take responsibility for a creative space in school;
- Making links between this space (geographically attached, yet apart) and the school in order to develop creative approaches across the curriculum and make teaching more appropriate for young people.

Schools wishing to develop their own Room 13 have access to the experience, examples, support and inspiration of others (for instance, through the website www.room13scotland.com); the chapter below is only one of a number of schools throughout the UK that have now followed the model.

Who's who?

- *Mike Fairclough:* Headteacher of West Rise Junior School, Eastbourne
- *Neil Small:* Newly appointed deputy head, West Rise Junior School
- *Karen Stephens:* Teaching assistant, West Rise Junior School
- *Abbie Norris:* Artist in residence, West Rise Junior School
- *Sara Bragg:* Researcher, the Open University

This chapter was compiled by the editor, with contributions from Sara Bragg. In constructing the chapter we drew on Neil Small's writing about the project for a master's course in education that he undertook and Sara's research in the school as part of the Creative Partnerships funded research project, 'Youth Voice in the work of Creative Partnerships'.

The school context and key issues

- *Name:* West Rise Junior School
- *Location:* Eastbourne, UK
- *Age range:* 7–11
- *No. on roll:* Approximately 250

The Room 13 in this chapter is situated in a junior school in a southern seaside town. The school has just over 250 children and higher than average numbers of children on free school meals or with statements of special needs. Physically, Room 13 is adjacent to but separate from the main school building, occupying the first floor of a two-storey studio converted from a disused caretaker's residence. It was proposed by the current headteacher when he applied for the headship, and so was in effect approved by the selection panel in appointing him.

The artist in residence is a computer-based visual media artist. The studio has two Apple Macs with animation software, linked to a permanently set up video camera; another digital camera available for use; and various other materials, from clay to paint, charcoal to Modroc. Children choose activities when they enter the room, often working in pairs or groups, across year groups, sometimes alone.

Funding was initially obtained from Creative Partnerships to pay the artist in residence. However, the school is committed to retaining the initiative and therefore helped to fund the artist initially for a year after. Room 13 is now self-financed following successful bids by the artist in residence.

Room 13 is open for two days of the week. During lesson time, two children from each class may request permission to attend (ensuring a maximum of sixteen students present), with the class teacher generally in control of the process by which attendance is decided. Occasionally the artist works on specific projects with larger groups of children from one class, although this is never likely to be more than sixteen students. It is also open at lunchtime for anyone who wants to go, although in principle committee members could restrict access if it becomes too crowded.

In the years following the headteacher's appointment, over half the teaching staff left and were replaced. Support for creativity and understanding of the Room 13 initiative were key qualities actively sought in new appointments. The school now has a completely new senior management team, all of whom are involved in realising the vision of Room 13 and developing creativity within the curriculum and other areas of the school. The senior management team were particularly interested in notions of creativity that foregrounded the creation of a physical and social environment for and through creativity, and the merit in working with teacher beliefs and values.[2]

Timeline

The process of setting up Room 13 was a necessarily long one as it required structural as well as relational changes to be made within school:

- *Early 2005:* Idea presented to staff and other stakeholders.
- *2005–6:* Discussion of the idea with parents, teachers and other stakeholders.
- *Summer term of 2006:* Assemblies held presenting the idea to the children.
- *September 2006:* Committee selected.
- *Autumn term 2006–7:* Three-day visit to another Room 13 in Fort William in Scotland, involving the committee members and their families, the headteacher, deputy headteacher, another teaching assistant and the artist (who was not at that stage the artist in residence). The group shared their experiences at a staff meeting.
- *Spring term 2006:* Gradual introduction of the Room 13 concept. The artist ran morning workshops with each year group, and the studio was then opened to the same groups in the afternoon.
- *April 2007:* Official opening of Room 13. It has been running two days a week since then, and the ground floor studio space has been used for other more focused 'creative' projects.

The role of young people

The first committee of eight children was selected by staff following a 'competition' inviting children to imagine what Room 13 might look like. The teaching assistant, artist in residence and deputy head met with the children initially to explain the different roles within the committee. The adults chose a treasurer by setting a maths problem, but otherwise the children allotted tasks amongst themselves. Their decision to appoint, as chair, a Year 5 child (aged 9–10) surprised the adults, who had assumed that the responsibility required a Year 6 pupil (that is, the highest year in the school and the pupils are aged 10–11); the chair's success in her role further challenged an unthinking link between biological age and capacity.

Is this link between biological age and capacity something that you recognise? Do you think this might present barriers to young people's participation?

Subsequently, new committee members were chosen by previous post-holders, mainly on the basis of their involvement and interest in Room 13 – that is, children who most often used Room 13 were more likely to get involved in running it.

Committee members attend a weekly Room 13 after-school club and hold committee meetings once or twice every week during a school assembly. They are responsible for managing a budget, ordering stock, deciding on purchases of new stock and equipment, tidying the studio, communicating ideas and events, contacting other creative practitioners in the area when appropriate, and organising committee meetings. At the time of writing, four years into the initiative the extent of their involvement in the business and 'enterprise' elements of Room 13 is still relatively under-developed. The adults involved also acknowledge the extent to which the young people require active support and resourcing from them in order to work effectively. Even maintaining the studio as a well-organised and relatively orderly space has presented challenges, as children have not always done this spontaneously.

> The adults acknowledge that young people 'require active support and resourcing.' What are the implications of this in a school setting?

All students have a major role in 'selling' the concept of Room 13 to adults. One significant audience is of course the parents of children in the school, who note the spontaneous, voluble enthusiasm expressed by those who have spent time in Room 13 during their school day. The committee members in addition have travelled to conferences and other events to present and discuss their work. They also regularly run assemblies. Some children became more confident in asking for help and in talking to people they might not usually approach as a result of this. These experiences have helped to change some young people's views of themselves as this committee member (aged 10) suggested:

> Room 13 has changed my whole personality and how I think of people like [other people on the committee] 'cause if this wasn't here I would still be at that 'Oh my god, I'm so scared they might not like me', but now you've got meetings with other people and people come up to you and say, 'Hey can you help me with this?' and you're not scared to go up to them and say you can help them.
>
> (Room 13 committee member, aged 10, quoted in
> Neil Small's master's dissertation)

> Committee members have been able to present and discuss their work in a variety of contexts which seems to have been beneficial to them. Consider how you might widen the 'audiences' that the young people in your school are able to reach. What different skills and approaches might be required by different audiences?

The artist in residence

The school was initially interested in employing an artist to work in partnership with it as it was felt that she would bring professional expertise that would complement and extend creative learning and teaching in the school. The artist in residence has been both a crucial resource and a major influence in how Room 13 has developed in this context. She had worked in the school on earlier projects, and then participated in the school visit to an established Room 13. She found it so impressive that she stayed on to help the school's initiative, and over the years has engaged in rich discussions with senior managers about how children learn, about her role, how she relates to the children, and how best to help the committee.

Whilst the artist did not have a formal teaching background, she was committed to taking a non-interventionist but 'facilitative' role. Her role as a professional artist was important. For instance, if children approached her with a creative idea in mind, she did not pass judgement on the concept, but offered her professional artistic expertise to help them realise it. In relation to learning she felt that the focus in Room 13 should be on young people developing their own ideas, exploring their own strengths and working to their own timetable. She came to believe that:

> Teaching is about exploring and sharing, being willing to continue learning. It is about enthusiasm and expression. It is about using the teacher [or in this case the artist] as a resource using their own interests and strengths, then giving them the skills to share that information with the children, bringing it to life.
> (Abbie Norris, quoted in Neil Small's master's dissertation, 2008)

How do you respond to this vision of teaching and learning? Do you have an opportunity to work in this way in your setting? Would you want to?

The original motive behind employing an artist to work with the children and teachers was to inspire and challenge young people and school staff to experiment with new ideas and ways of working. Whilst this seemed to be effective with young people in a variety of ways, teachers were less convinced of the value of Room 13 in influencing their practices.

Curriculum change: teaching and learning

The aim of Room 13 was to encourage teachers to think about *what* was being taught and *how* it was being taught, to make teaching more appropriate to the children. Enabling teachers to reflect on how children learn in Room 13 was seen as a way to encourage discussion about how children might learn throughout the school. The school looked to the document 'All our Futures'[3] to help them plan their journey into creative learning. The aspects that senior managers at West Rise particularly liked were around nurturing teachers' creative abilities and the notion of creative approaches supporting the development of the 'whole child'. They were also intrigued about the notion of 'flow'[4] and specifically whether a creative space could change the way young people engage with a creative activity.

However, because teachers are not involved or even present in the space, they have had limited opportunities to learn from what goes on there. In addition, whilst they appreciate how much children value Room 13, they consider that it operates under such different conditions (e.g. in terms of group size) that it has little relevance to their own practice.

What aspects of the Room 13 approach might be transferable into classroom teaching and learning? How might this be facilitated?

The physical 'space' of Room 13

Children and adults talked a lot about the value of 'being in the space' rather than of the work they produced. Pupils felt that they owned the space themselves, a sense of autonomy perhaps reinforced by the physical detachment of the studio from the main school building. In addition the young people on the committee were instrumental in designing the space themselves, creating an environment very different from a classroom. In fact, a visiting parent remarked that the studio looked like 'a child's bedroom':

Figure 7.1 Room 13

Now [Room 13 is] all colourful, it's like a child's room that they've just done themselves. It's all splattered around, you just feel like a child again.

(Parent, quoted in Neil Small's Master's dissertation, 2008)

Adults observed that children gradually developed a different 'way of being' in the Room 13 space. The creation of a marginal space for creativity within school may be particularly important for young people as schools, and indeed young people's lives in general, become increasingly regulated and monitored.

Are there 'risks' in setting up a space in school that is self consciously 'different' to the rest of the school? How might these 'risks' be overcome?

Different rules and conventions

In Room 13 children relished the non-compulsory nature of their activities there, in contrast to their classroom experience:

If you're in school, it's almost like you don't have individuality, you have to … do a certain thing, but here you don't have to follow certain guidelines …

(Room 13 participant, aged 9,
quoted in Neil Small's Master's dissertation, 2008)

Another child agreed that there are different rules and conventions in Room 13 suggesting,

You go there to be yourself, 'cause in class you've got to behave, be quiet, work. But in there you can talk, talk to people and have a laugh when you're doing something […] in the school you have rules, here, you have rules but they're not as strict as they are in the classroom.

(Child aged 9, quoted in Neil Small's Master's dissertation, 2008)

This aspect also struck a researcher:

Two boys rush in with a photocopy of a giant ruler, which they then set about gluing to the walls. I observe my reaction – I'm initially shocked to see them doing this: they haven't even asked permission from an adult! Then I realise that of course, if this is their studio, they can do what they like in it, and they are simply demonstrating their sense of ownership and entitlement. I look around and begin to notice other photocopies stuck directly onto the walls, including some lovely, life-size ones of children upside down. So in a very real way I am reminded that this is a different kind of space, where different rules apply.

(Sara Bragg, Research fieldnotes, March 2008)

The more relaxed rules in Room 13 offered them a chance, argued a teacher, 'to experiment and to be creative in a safe environment'. The artist also suggests that Room 13 is a space where young people can feel safe to express an opinion, idea, experience, notion or feeling because there are no right or wrong answers. In addition, the artist believes that the young people are treated as equals in the studio.

It seems that in Room 13 young people feel more able to express themselves, partly because they have some jurisdiction over the space and are therefore repositioned in relationship to the adults in school.

Peer-to-peer collaboration

The different rules and freedom to choose activities also encouraged greater collaboration and cooperation with peers. Children mix year groups and work with pupils in other classes in a way that they are not able to do in the main body of the school. Young people showed that they were capable of lengthy, highly elaborated exchanges amongst themselves, usually focused on solving problems related to creative effects or aims and how to achieve them in practice. These were very different from the short 'Initiation, response, feedback' (IRF[5]) exchanges required by classroom practice. Children could exhibit extraordinary focus and concentration on tasks that enthused them in this way (see Csikszentmihalyi, 1996).

Would it be possible to create this kind of environment in a 'normal' classroom? What would be the challenges in doing so – and possible solutions?

Process or product: artistic quality?

The committee have decided that all work produced in Room 13 belongs to Room 13 and no work is taken home. This came about because the committee felt that children were using too many resources to produce work of little artistic value. As an example, children were frequently making cards for their family. This rule was brought in to enable the work to have more of a focus on process. Although products also remain important for the children, the rule has helped them to focus on working on pieces of art for longer periods of time. The artist can now better promote critical reflection and learning on how to improve and develop. Finished products, therefore, are not the only, or indeed the most important criteria in judging the 'success' of the Room 13 initiative.

The artist claims that, 'we influence each other's work and exchange ideas and criticisms. We are collaborators in Room 13 and everyone's ideas are valuable'. However, other adults including teachers in the school have sometimes expressed disappointment at the quality of the work children have produced given the expertise that is potentially available to them. The artist therefore has a difficult role in working out how to use her own skills helpfully and to draw on the responses of other children so that 'they can learn to criticise and to be criticised by others in a nurturing way.'

How do you view the relationship between process and product in creative learning initiatives? Do you think that increased attention on the 'process' will inevitably result in the creation of a better 'quality' of product? What mechanisms and practices may need to be adopted to create a better chance of this outcome?

Key learning points

Benefits of working in a creative space that is marginal to school

Children designed the studio space themselves and displays were predominantly of their own work. These displays were used as inspiration for other children using the space. Different rules and conventions applied in this space, that for many children encouraged a feeling of 'being safe', that in turn led to more experimentation and different relationships with adults and their peers.

Reconfigurations of power

Putting children in charge of running Room 13 challenged notions of their capabilities – for both adults and the children themselves.

Linking Room 13 with school practices

Room 13 has not yet been able to influence teaching and learning in the rest of the school in specific quantifiable ways. Arguably it may even produce polarisation – with Room 13 being seen as the 'creative' space and classrooms as its opposite.

Professional development questions

The pupils enjoy the freedom and the sense of being valued as an individual that they feel when in Room 13 which they do not seem to feel in the main body of the school. Pupil voice is increasingly playing a part in moderating and self review in schools. However often spaces of participation are marginalised in schools in this way. What are the barriers to embedding this type of youth participation into school structures and practices? And what might be possible solutions?

Directed learning or giving knowledge is easier than self-directed learning to quantify, as the starting and ending points are clearer. Learning that takes less foreseen direction and operates in more of a free flowing way has the outcome as its least important part, and the process of learning as the key to the learning experience. What are the difficulties in adopting this style of learning in your school and how could they be overcome?

There were difficulties in this school in involving teachers in Room 13 which meant that the project did not achieve its objective of encouraging teachers to make teaching more appropriate to the children. How might this project have been structured differently to allow for more teacher involvement? What might have been the advantages and disadvantages of this?

Notes

1   See Jeff Adams 'Room 13 and the contemporary practice of Artist-Learners', in J. Sefton-Green (2011) *The Routledge International Handbook of Creative Learning*. London: Routledge.

2   Beetlestone, F. (1998) *Creative Children, Imaginative Teaching*. Buckingham: Open University Press.

3   National Advisory Committee for Creative and Cultural Education, *All Our Futures: Creativity, Culture, Education,* May 1999. 'All our Futures' was a report made to government by a committee led by Ken Robinson on the creative and cultural development of young people through formal and informal education: to take stock of current provision and to make proposals for principles, policies and practice. Downloadable at www.cypni.org.uk/downloads/allourfutures.pdf

4   Mihaly Csikszentmihalyi (1996). *Creativity: Flow and the Psychology of Discovery and Invention*. New York: Harper Perennial.

5   Initiation, Response, Feedback (IRF). The IRF model described by van Lier (1996) consists of the teacher initiating talk (almost always via a question), the pupil responding and the teacher evaluating the response (i.e. providing feedback judgement).

References

Adams, J. (2011) 'Room 13 and the contemporary practice of Artist-Learners', in J. Sefton-Green, P. Thomson, K. Jones and L. Bresler (eds) *The Routledge International Handbook of Creative Learning*. London: Routledge.

Beetlestone, F. (1998) *Creative Children, Imaginative Teaching*. Buckingham: Open University Press.

Csikszentmihalyi, Mihaly (1996) *Creativity: Flow and the Psychology of Discovery and Invention*. New York: Harper Perennial.

van Lier, L. (1996) 'Contingency' *in Interaction in the Language Curriculum: Awareness, Autonomy and Authenticity*. London: Longman.

Appendix
Staff development and resources

Professional development sessions

These sessions can be used for whole staff INSET sessions or smaller group work amongst staff, or with young people. You might want to consider including young people in these whole school INSET sessions or asking a creative practitioner to facilitate a session.

Access and inclusion

Purpose/aim　To use the case studies to consider issues of access and inclusion in relation to young people's participation in school decision making and creativity.

Time　1½ hours

Participants　Whole staff (could include young people)

Outline of activity　Using the case studies, staff work in small groups to explore how other schools have included young people in school decision making. In particular considering the questions:

- Who was involved?
- How did they come to be involved? How was this viewed by others?

Resources　Copies of the case studies, handouts of Fielding's model (see Box A.1), flipchart paper, pens.

Instructions

- Split staff into six groups. Each group has a copy of one of the case studies.
- Each group reads their case study to answer the questions: Which young people were involved? How did they come to be involved? How might this be viewed by other young people? Write notes on flipchart paper in three columns and remind each group member that they need to record or remember their answers.

Work out where you would place the activity on Fielding's model of student participation.

- 'Jigsaw' the groups so that six new groups are formed with one member from each group. These new groups discuss their findings from the six case studies in relation to the three questions and Fielding's model.
- These groups consider student participation practices in their own school in which young people are excluded, or are hardly included. Groups consider why this is the case and possible solutions.
- Plenary: INSET facilitator encourages groups to share findings and identify one group of young people who have not been included who they feel would benefit from a creative approach.

Further development

Using the findings from this INSET assign a small group of staff and pupils to work together to plan and implement a creative participation activity that includes the identified group of young people in school decision making.

Box A.1: Fielding's model

- students as data source – in which staff utilise information about student progress and well-being;
- students as active respondents – in which staff invite student dialogue and discussion to deepen learning/professional decisions;
- students as co-enquirers – in which staff take a lead role with high-profile, active student support;
- students as knowledge creators – in which students take lead roles with active staff support;
- students as joint authors – in which students and staff decide on a joint course of action together;
- intergenerational learning as participatory democracy – in which there is a shared commitment to/responsibility for the common good.

Adult–youth relationships

Purpose/aim To identify aspects of positive, collaborative relationships between adults and young people in participation activities and to consider creative solutions to overcoming constraints on collaborative relationships.

Time 1½ hours

Participants Whole staff (could include young people)

Outline of activity Using the case studies from the book, staff will identify elements that contributed to 'positive' relations of participation between adults and young people. Staff will consider what educators might learn from creative practitioners.

Resources   Photocopies of the case studies, flipchart paper and stand, pens, two colours of Post-it notes.

Instructions

- Ask all participants to write down two statements each about relationships between young people and teachers. These statements can be either 1) true to the school *or* 2) deliberately controversial. Group leader collects the statements and asks staff to stand up somewhere in the room. Group leader randomly picks a statement from their pile and reads it out. Participants are asked to move to an area of the room depending on how far they agree or disagree with the statement. The group leader then asks several people to explain why they have chosen to stand where they have. Repeat as often as time allows.

- Six groups to be formed. Each group is to read one of the case studies to identify elements that contributed to positive relationships between adults and young people (NB these elements might be related to behaviour but may also include other aspects related to the project contexts or the 'spaces' created on the projects). Each group is to write these elements on Post-it notes. Choose another colour of Post-it note and write what (if anything) they feel teachers might be able to learn from the approaches of creative practitioners.

- Group leader collects the Post-it notes and places them in two columns on a flipchart paper. Group facilitator leads a plenary discussion.

- Back in small groups discuss whether they feel there are constraints in implementing these elements of teacher–youth relationships in their own practice. List the constraints and identify creative solutions to at least two of these constraints.

Further development

Consider working with young people and creative practitioners to action plan how to bring one idea into practice.

Ask a creative practitioner (perhaps in collaboration with a group of teachers and young people) to run an INSET session to work further on overcoming some of the constraints identified by staff.

Interrogating current practice

Purpose/aim   To interrogate student participation initiatives in school and ask critical questions of current practice. To consider whether creative approaches to participation could improve current practice.

Time   2½ hours

Participants   A small group of staff interested in or already involved in student participation – if possible a creative practitioner.

Outline of activity Staff will map current student participation activities in the school and ask critical questions about it. Working with a creative practitioner or another facilitator, staff will consider how creative approaches might enhance student participation activities.

Resources Hand-outs of the 'critical questions' at the end of the introduction of this book (pp. 14–15), flipchart paper and pens *or* creative practitioner 'tools'

Instructions

- Each staff member describes their involvement or interest in student participation, and briefly describes activities in the school.
- Staff work together to 'represent' the current student voice activities in the school in whatever form they wish (or as the creative practitioner working with them suggests).
- Staff use the questions provided on the hand-out to consider current practices in the school.
- Creative practitioner works with this staff group to consider how creative approaches might be utilised to improve or enhance current practices in the school.

Further developments

Work with the creative practitioner to plan and deliver a creative participation project.

Considering young people

Purpose To ask staff to consider their own views and expectations of young people in the school.

Time 1 hour

Participants Whole staff

Outline of activity Staff to consider their own views of expectations of young people and their capabilities.

Resources Flipchart paper and pens, six case studies.

Instructions

- Participants form groups (4 or 5 in each group). Consider a moment when young people surprised you with their capabilities or skills. Share and discuss these moments. What was it that surprised you?
- Read one case study in each group and make a note of the kinds of activities young people were involved in and the capabilities and expertise they have demonstrated. Does anything surprise them in relation to the capabilities of young people?
- Then consider and answer (on flipchart paper) the question 'what is the image of a child that we hold in this school?'

Further development

Plan some further work with young people (and possibly creative practitioners) to begin to redefine adults' views of young people's capabilities.

Consider the 'Funds of knowledge' approach to young people and their families by reading the work of Norma González, Luis C. Moll and Cathy Amanti.[1] Their work suggests that teachers should work with young people and their families and communities as learners, gaining first hand experience as researchers of their communities in order to document their existing competence and knowledge. How could you develop this kind of an approach within your school?

Youth forum

Purpose To find out more about young people's views on their participation in school.

Time 2 hours

Participants A group of young people – preferably a diverse group including some who have been involved in participation initiatives and others who have not.

Outline of activity A 'youth forum' event that asks young people to consider responses to various statements concerning youth participation at school.

Resources Statements related to participation printed out large on A3 paper (see below), different coloured stickers, recording device.

Instructions

- Start with an ice-breaker or speed dating activity to help young people to get to know each other. For example, you could try a speed dating activity where students get up and find people they don't know to discuss questions such as: 'What's your favourite TV programme or film?' Find two things in common. Who is your favourite celebrity or actor? What's your favourite place in school? What's your favourite place outside school?
- Then ask young people to answer the question, 'If this school was an animal what kind of animal would it be?' (You will get some interesting responses that might tell you a lot about how young people feel about the school.)
- Ask young people to work as one whole group or several smaller groups to look at the statements and place coloured dots next to the ones they agree with and discuss the questions together.
- Lead a whole group discussion concerning their responses to these statements.
- Try to record the discussion which could then be used at staff or senior management meetings to inform future practice.

Further development

Continue to work with this group of young people in planning student participation activities in the school.

Use their responses as a stimulus for staff discussion.

Box A.2   Statements for youth forum

1   Schools and teachers have no idea what young people are really like.

- Schools and teachers don't know much about what we do outside school.
- Schools and teachers don't know much about how we communicate with each other, or what we enjoy/value.
- Schools are too focused on exams.

Discuss: What kinds of things do teachers need to know about young people's lives to improve schools?

How could schools change to connect better with young people?

2   Schools often choose a few students and give them a lot of resources and support so that schools can *say* they listen to young people …

… but that doesn't necessarily make things any better for (or make any difference to) the rest of the students, or to relationships in schools.

Discuss: It would be difficult for schools to listen to all the students in the school.

Some young people feel they never get included.

Some young people get most of the attention and others are left out.

3   Young people need to learn how to talk in a way that adults understand, and will listen to.

Young people need special training to learn to communicate on a level with adults.

Adults should learn more about how young people communicate in order to be able to listen properly.

4   It's really good when adults who aren't teachers come into school to work with us.

Discuss: What kind of things do they do/where do they work with you? Who are they?

How do they work with you? (Is it different from how your teachers work with you? How?)

5   Schools say they want to listen to young people, but they don't ask us about the things that matter most to us.

Discuss: Some students say they feel labelled by streaming (being placed in bottom sets), or are seen as 'dumb' because of the way they dress, but they don't get a chance to challenge that.

What are the things that matter to you, in school, outside school?

Additional resources

In this section you will find some additional resources that may be helpful in planning projects and continuing professional development activities in your schools.

A checklist for creative participation

This checklist suggests some key considerations and questions that may aid planning and delivery of creative participation activities.

Pre-participation

- Spend time establishing parameters and purpose: for example, is the focus too wide to lead to specific actions, or too narrow to seem worthwhile and significant? Does it give young people a genuine role? How open-ended are the outcomes, or are they already confined to a choice between a narrow range of options?
- What will young people gain from their involvement? Is it in their interest to be involved?
- Practical concerns – who will be involved? If they are chosen, who chooses them and how will this be perceived? How might you include marginalised groups, such as minority ethnic children or those with disabilities?
- What divisions/differences exist between the young people and how will you deal with this diversity?
- What about time scales?
- What kind of adult support might be required?
- How will it be integrated into school systems and ethos and into local and global networks and practices?
- How will you deal with ethical issues such as confidentiality and anonymity?

Focus of the participation

- Is the topic one that appeals to young people?
- If there are limits, communicate these clearly to those involved from the beginning.
- How will you explain the purpose of their participation, their responsibilities and role within it? How long will it take, its funding, and the consequences and implications of expressing their views?

Post participation

- What will happen to young people's views once they have been collected? How will they be communicated and disseminated, and by whom? What kind of feedback loops and spaces for dialogue will be established? Is there a commitment from the relevant people to providing a response, even if nothing can be acted upon immediately?

- Who is the audience and how does this affect communication of the findings? For instance, traditional approaches such as written reports can reach a number of diverse and broad audiences; however creative methods such as workshops, video or audio recordings or other feedback events may be more appropriate for young people.

- How will young people be involved in communicating findings?

- Involving young people can have a strong impact on adult audiences, but care should be taken not to put young people in difficult situations, such as those where they receive negative responses.

- How will you create a space for dialogue to take place at this stage? This may be necessary partly in order to clarify the meaning of the findings, and partly to allow for disagreements and differences of opinion to be aired and compromises negotiated (ideas adapted from Bragg, 2010).

Models of participation

Perhaps the best known of these is Roger Hart's 'ladder of participation' (Hart, 1992).[2]

In this model the lowest (non-participatory) rungs involve forms of manipulation, decoration or tokenism where young people do not have important roles and are sometimes actively exploited for adults' agendas. In higher rungs young people may take on information-giving roles within adult-initiated projects, or 'consultation' work. The highest rungs suggest shared decision-making on adult initiated projects, projects initiated and directed by young people with support from adults, or youth-initiated projects with shared decision-making. There is some debate concerning the importance of dialogue versus young people's autonomy in these higher rungs (Bragg, 2010). However, the model has proven useful for organisations to assess the place of young people in the work that they do.

Other models have been specifically designed for use in schools. For example, Flutter and Rudduck's (2004) model for student voice (and particularly student as researcher initiatives) within which different forms of participation are placed according to the levels of child-led decision making or initiation at different stages of the research process. This model starts with 'no pupil consultation' and moves through four stages: listening to pupils, pupils as active participants, pupils as researchers and finally pupils as fully active participants and co-researchers (see Flutter and Rudduck's model in Box 4.2 on p. 57).

Shier's (2001)[3] model called 'pathways to participation' is also a useful resource that foregrounds the role of adults in supporting young people's participation work in schools.

A.1: Staff development and resources figure: pathways to participation

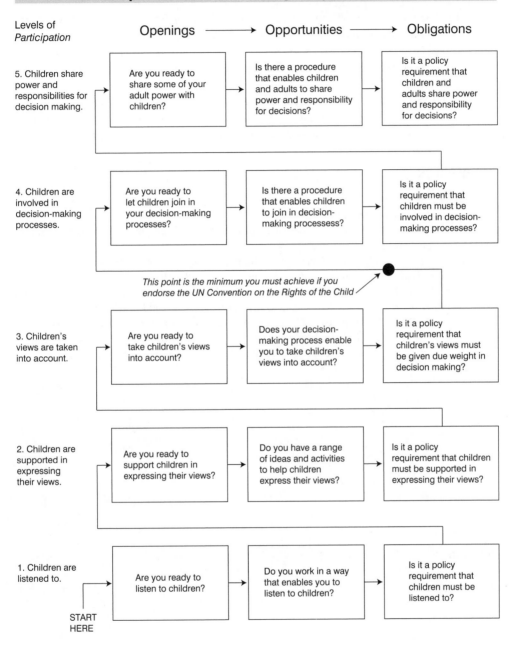

Levels of *Participation*

Openings ⟶ Opportunities ⟶ Obligations

5. Children share power and responsibilities for decision making.

Are you ready to share some of your adult power with children?

Is there a procedure that enables children and adults to share power and responsibility for decisions?

Is it a policy requirement that children and adults share power and responsibility for decisions?

4. Children are involved in decision-making processes.

Are you ready to let children join in your decision-making processes?

Is there a procedure that enables children to join in decision-making processess?

Is it a policy requirement that children must be involved in decision-making processes?

This point is the minimum you must achieve if you endorse the UN Convention on the Rights of the Child

3. Children's views are taken into account.

Are you ready to take children's views into account?

Does your decision-making process enable you to take children's views into account?

Is it a policy requirement that children's views must be given due weight in decision making?

2. Children are supported in expressing their views.

Are you ready to support children in expressing their views?

Do you have a range of ideas and activities to help children express their views?

Is it a policy requirement that children must be supported in expressing their views?

1. Children are listened to.

Are you ready to listen to children?

Do you work in a way that enables you to listen to children?

Is it a policy requirement that children must be listened to?

START HERE

107

Notes

1. N. González, L. Moll and C. Amanti (2005) *Funds of Knowledge: Theorizing Practices in Households, Communities, and Classrooms*. London: Routledge.
2. R. Hart. (1992) *Children's Participation: From Tokenism to Citizenship*. Innocenti essays no. 4, Florence: UNICEF. The model is available online at http://www.freechild.org/ladder.htm
3. H. Shier (2001) Pathways to participation: openings, opportunities and obligations. A new model for enhancing children's participation in line with Article 12.1 of the United Nations Convention on the Rights of the Child. *Children and Society*, 15: 107–17.

References

Bragg, S. (2010) (2nd edn) *Consulting Young People: A Literature Review*. London: Creativity, Culture and Education.

Flutter, J. and Rudduck, J. (2004). *Consulting Pupils. What's in It for Schools?* London: RoutledgeFalmer.

González, N., Moll, L. and Amanti, C. (2005) *Funds of Knowledge: Theorizing Practices in Households, Communities, and Classrooms*. London: Routledge.

Hart, R. (1992) *Children's Participation: From Tokenism to Citizenship*. Innocenti essays No. 4, Florence: UNICEF. Available at http://www.freechild.org/ladder.htm

Shier, H. (2001) Pathways to participation: openings, opportunities and obligations. A new model for enhancing children's participation in line with Article 12.1 of the United Nations Convention on the Rights of the Child. *Children and Society*, 15: 107–17.

Index